The
Guilty
Gardener

The Guilty Gardener

Annabel Christie

Illustrated by Iris Rushbrooke

Matador
Unit E2 Airfield Business Park,
Harrison Road, Market Harborough,
Leicestershire. LE16 7UL
Tel: 0116 279 2299
Email: books@troubador.co.uk
Web: www.troubador.co.uk/matador
Twitter: @matadorbooks

ISBN 978 1803135 120

British Library Cataloguing in Publication Data.
A catalogue record for this book is available from the British Library.

Printed and bound by CPI Group (UK) Ltd, Croydon, CR0 4YY
Typeset in 11pt Minion Pro by Troubador Publishing Ltd, Leicester, UK

Matador is an imprint of Troubador Publishing Ltd

In memory of my father – a true naturalist

The earth,
the air, the land and
the water are on
loan from our children.
We have to hand over to
them
at least as it was handed
over to us

Mahatma Gandhi

CONTENTS

ONE

THE LETTER

It was my father's letter that finally did it, rediscovering it after all these years. It was like a thunderbolt to my conscience, a silent plea from the grave reminding me of my magical childhood garden, broken promises and my failure to make amends.

I knew at once I had to act. I couldn't prevaricate any longer and watch helplessly as everything my father strove for, everything he believed in and once taught me, fell asunder and was lost forever. I would put nature first again and do everything in my power to help save our precious wildlife before it was too late. And I would do this in the one place I knew I could make a difference – my own neglected garden. I owed it to Dad, I owed it to the children but, most of all, I owed it to nature.

When he passed away three years ago from cancer, my dear father left me with a gaping hole in my heart and a mountain of regrets. Throughout his seventy-seven years on this earth, he had always put nature first in everything he sought to do and although he would never have admitted it – he was far too conservative for that – he was an activist at heart, a fervent environmentalist who would have fought tooth and nail to protect our natural heritage.

If he were here today, he would be devastated by the catastrophe unfolding in our natural world, and the continuing threat to our planet from climate change and other man-made disasters. He would be out there campaigning for a wilder Britain, and I am certain he would be telling me, over and over again, to get off my lazy, negligent backside and rewild too.

His letter could easily have not been found. It was tucked inside the gilt-edged front cover of an antiquated butterfly book and slipped onto my lap like a *billet doux* as I lifted the old, heavy tome from the coffin depths of my father's leather-bound trunk. It was the third anniversary of his death and the first time I had dared explore the musty interior of his school chest, curious but nervous to uncover what childhood secrets it might hold. When I prised open the trunk's metal clasps, I was amazed to discover it was packed with my father's precious collection of wildlife and gardening books, each one a reminder of my nature-filled past.

The tome which hid the letter was my father's first edition of the *Natural History of British Butterflies* by the renowned lepidopterist, Frederick William Frohawk. Dad and I had often shared it together when I was still his little girl and held in nature's thrall. Snuggled on his knee, in the light of the fire, I would marvel at the exquisite, intricate drawings of Frohawk's different butterflies while he related, in minute detail, the life stages of each species and their individual characteristics, always leaving me intrigued and eager for more.

Moments like this brought me close to my father and inspired a childhood passion for nature that defined our special relationship in the first decade and a half of my life.

Dad realised early on that we shared this love of wildlife and would often invite me to help him in the garden. I readily accepted, following him like a lapdog through the jungle of long meadow grass and wildflowers that cloaked our back garden, eager to listen and learn from the great master as he clipped his roses or collected seeds to pot later. In return for imparting his botanical knowledge, he got me sowing and hoeing vegetables each spring in his resplendent Victorian glass greenhouse, planting flowers for butterflies, bees and caterpillars, building log piles for beetles and lizards and making cosy shelters for foxes and hedgehogs. I was never bored when I was with him but in the rare moments I was at a loose end, Dad would fling me a packet of wildflower seeds and instruct me to scatter them liberally, saying that each seed was a tiny grain of magic that, with the first warm rays of sunshine, would alchemise into food for hungry pollinators. I could barely wait for the snow to melt and the advent of summer when the seeds' tiny flowerheads sprouted through the grass, transforming our garden into a kaleidoscope of vibrant colour and insect life.

I loved Dad's eternal enthusiasm for nature, and perhaps his greatest legacy to me and my older brother, Simon, was teaching us that we were part of nature too, simple animals just like the badger, the fox and the hare.

'Our relationship with nature is actually more important than any other,' he said to me one summer's afternoon in 1977 as we sat together on the terrace of our family home in Kent watching a small mouse nibbling some wild strawberries. 'Break the link, and we all suffer.' He drew a circular diagram then, like a teacher would draw at school, showing me how mice eat insects and plants (even fungi) and how animals higher up the food chain – the fox, owl, hawk and snake – rely on the mice and other small creatures to sustain them. 'Even the least exciting lichen on a rotting tree trunk will be nectar for some garden insect or become nesting material for a bird. Every living organism in the garden has its part to play in the rich tapestry of life,' he proudly told me.

Our green odyssey continued in harmony for most of my childhood and early teens until, around my fifteenth birthday, I made the grand gesture that I didn't want to help him anymore in the garden; I was through with potting plants and sowing seeds and no longer cared as much about the wildlife. I had better things to do; it was 1980 and I wanted to be out partying with school friends, having fun and savouring my full quota of teenage kicks. My days of being my father's lapdog, grounded at home and in the garden, were well and truly over.

I know he was devastated because he retreated to the sanctity of his greenhouse for what seemed like an eternity and never once asked me to help him again in the garden. I felt a little ashamed of letting him down but not enough to change course. Then, a few years later, after I had completed my degree and was on the cusp of leaving home to go travelling, he sent me the letter. It was the first proper correspondence he had ever written to me and the one and only time I remember him letting his feelings truly show. I kept it for many years in a drawer in my childhood bedroom in Kent and then, after he died and my mother moved closer to me, it travelled with her in the antiquated trunk.

I lift the handwritten missive carefully out of its envelope and reread it in the hazy morning light.

The Old Coach House
Kent

October 5th, 1988

My Dearest Annabel,

You may remember that you wrote a nature diary in 1978 when you were 12 years old. I kept it safe because although nature and gardening are not top of your agenda right now, I'm sure they will take centre stage again when you are older and realise what you have missed.

I wanted to write to you because I fear we are losing the wonderful world you were so fortunate to enjoy as a child. Our never-ending pursuit of so-called 'progress' is pushing our planet to its outer limits and I fear it will collapse completely if we continue on this road.

I hope you will always hold wildlife close to your heart, just as you did as a child, and do everything in your power to protect it. Whatever you do, never forget how precious nature once was to you and how you marvelled at the changing seasons, our glorious birds (do you remember the waxwings?), the indigo cornflowers and delicate, crimson poppies that bloomed in the fields behind the house; our ancient oak that gave us shelter and acorns, and all the tiny creatures that enthralled your young mind. Don't lose the child inside you, dear Annabel, and never forget that nature brings enduring peace and happiness.

I know you are jetting off soon to India with friends on an adventure of a lifetime so I thought you might appreciate these wise words from the great Mahatma Gandhi to set you on your way:

*'Any number of experiments
is too small and no sacrifice
is too great for attaining
sympathy with nature.'*

Much Love, Dad

TWO

GUILT

Each word was carefully chosen, each line a testament to my past. I feel the tears welling up just imagining my father writing those heartfelt words all those years ago. He would have been seated at his heavy Churchillian desk at the window in his study, surrounded by his nature books with sadness no doubt etched across his furrowed brow as he stared out at the beautiful garden I had so glibly rejected.

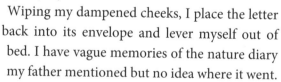

Wiping my dampened cheeks, I place the letter back into its envelope and lever myself out of bed. I have vague memories of the nature diary my father mentioned but no idea where it went. I don't remember seeing it in the trunk with his books or anywhere in my mother's new flat; I have to assume it got lost or left behind when my mother moved out of the family home. I reach for my pen and writing pad and scribble a brief message to the new owners of our old coach house, a young family with two small boys, asking if they would kindly check the outbuildings and attic above my childhood bedroom in case the diary got left behind. It's a long shot, I think, but worth a try. I would love to find it again.

After sealing the envelope, I go downstairs to the kitchen to feed Georgie, our black Flat-coated Retriever. She's lying upside down in her enormous brown cushioned bed, her four long legs erect like pokers and a cuspate head stretched backwards, but she springs into action when I enter the room, swaying her body affectionately in greeting. I sink my face into her soft fur and give her a long hug before getting myself a large cup of fresh coffee and sitting down at the kitchen table to plan my next move. Sooty, our dishevelled cat, comes sidling in from outside and, rather annoyingly, rubs her furry back against my leg, leaving an itchy trail of soft grey hair. 'I guess you need feeding too,' I sigh, flicking the fine down off my jeans.

Gazing absently out through the misted window at our back garden, dank and grey in the sombre morning light, I'm struck suddenly by the notable absence of birdlife. There's not a single bird flitting about in the trees or foraging for food on the ground, not even a fat pigeon. Twenty years ago, this wouldn't have been the case. When we first moved to our cottage in Oxfordshire, the garden was a veritable aviary, a haven for birds of all shapes and sizes. I remember my father remarking how lucky we were to have so many different songbird varieties. They were all here – blackbirds, warblers, finches, tits, thrushes, skylarks and blackcaps – but no longer. I can't believe the decline in just two decades and, more to the point, I can't believe it's taken me till now to notice.

Leaving my coffee half drunk, I grab Georgie's lead and stroll out the back door. I want to take a closer look at the garden. There's a rustle in one of the bushes but no bird emerges. There's nothing, a deathly void and silence with the only intermittent sound the distant drone of morning traffic making its way up and down our hill. I decide to abandon breakfast altogether and head straight out for my walk, calling to Georgie who has sniffed out our neighbour's cat under a large laurel bush and is barking frantically. I cross the finely cut front lawn, making my way towards the rickety wooden gate at the southern end of our garden. Beyond is a path that leads into a local cemetery and then down onto the Chiltern Way, and it's a route Georgie and I take most days when we're not meeting friends on the Ridgeway or walking by the Thames.

The manicured lawn is heavy with dew, a dazzling mass of sparkles in the morning sunlight, and the tall trees and dense bushes along our garden boundary are also reflecting the bright light, like giant sentries cloaked still in their sparkly green summer uniforms. It feels, on this mid-September morn, as if the garden is making one last stoic effort to ward off the inevitable fall into autumn. Nearing the gate, I am met with a faint, woody aroma of next door's bonfire, still lingering in the air, and all around there's a Monday morning calmness, broken only by the whoosh and rumble of a high-speed train coursing through the valley as it snakes its way from Oxford to London.

Before stepping through the gate, I stop to remove my coat and admire the view. It's a vista I love that's in constant flux depending on the time of year. Today, the undulating wheat fields are a sun blaze of fiery-orange, reminding me, rather bizarrely, of one of Picasso's muses, stretched out curvaceously in front of me as if on a giant canvas. Overhead, a large raptor is circling on the warm thermals, its witch-black wings and forked tail casting sinister shadows over the sunlit field as it searches for carrion or an unsuspecting vole. 'You're lucky,' I murmur, 'you've got the entire skyscape to yourself.'

On the surface, I sense that little has changed in this ancient valley since we moved here, but I know it has. There are fewer trees, wildflower meadows and hedgerows than there used to be, and the natural wildlife has dwindled too. I can't remember when I last heard the shrill whistle of a skylark overhead or caught a glimpse of a fleeing fox, hare or fallow deer and, despite being commonplace once, I've never ever seen or heard a nightingale or cuckoo heralding in the new season. Even a landscape, as eternally pretty and protected as ours, has failed to avoid the ravages of time and it's as if the wildlife, sensing change, has long since departed the valley.

Our garden wildlife has disappeared too.

When my husband, Ed, and I moved to the cottage with our two young children – Olivia was three then and Sam two – we weren't prepared for the acre-and-a-half of uncultivated jungle that we inherited and had no idea how to manage it. We came from a two-bed terraced house in London where the only outside space had been a neat, pint-sized courtyard where we grew a few random plants in pots.

Ed had a long commute to get used to and, after putting all our energy into the children, our jobs and our new home, we were both exhausted by the weekend. Neither of us had the verve or inclination to do anything active, least of all gardening. The easiest and most practical solution to managing our large and unwieldy plot was to downsize, which we did with remarkable speed. We halved the number of herbaceous borders, then swept away anything that required work or looked out of place including many mature trees, shrubs, hedges, wildflowers, even a pond. Worse still, we used gallons of weedkiller in the process, zapping any unfashionable plant or 'weed', irrespective of its wildlife value, and never once thought we might be damaging an ancient ecosystem. I certainly don't remember checking if birds were roosting or nesting when we removed the trees or if hedgehogs and other small mammals were sheltering in the scrubby undergrowth.

My father was horrified at the time and tried to ward us off our path of destruction, but his pleas fell on stony ground. My childhood passion for nature had long since departed and I was in no mood to change course, at least not then. Ed and I wanted a neat and manageable garden where the children could play safely and we could proudly entertain our London friends. We didn't want a messy jungle.

In place of these precious wildlife habitats, we sowed grass, acres of it, and I became known locally as the "Queen of Grass". Our cottage lawns were green and luscious and the envy of everyone we knew but, from a wildlife perspective, they were a disaster. We cut them so regularly and aggressively in summer that nothing grew, not even a tiny daisy.

Now, today, for the first time, I can see the broad, deep scars left on this once-thriving wildlife garden. By tidying away the mess and wildness, Ed and I have created a wide, neat space but lost the garden's beating heart and soul. We have lost everything that was essentially good for nature – the tantalising smells, the vibrant colours, the jungle madness, the rich diversity, the throbbing life. I try to remember when I last saw a pretty orchid or hedgehog or woke to the comforting hoot of an owl.

Probably not for over a decade.

I'm suddenly seized with panic, a heart-searing thud in the base of my gut that forces me to lean up against the side of the gate and compose myself. 'What have I done?' I moan, sinking my head into my hands as a sudden gust of wind whips up a cloud of grey-white smoke from the bonfire. It tastes stale and metallic against my tongue and makes me feel suddenly queasy.

Georgie looks up at me sheepishly, rubbing her soft back against my knee. I lean down to give her a comforting hug, and she licks my face affectionately. 'This is not your fault,' I say, staring into her pitiful doe eyes. Nothing is ever your fault. Then lifting my face to the sky, I call out at the top of my voice: 'Dad, if you're listening, if you're out there, I'm so sorry! I will make it up to you, I promise.'

Slipping through the gate, I'm awakened, all of a sudden, to a new sound, a beautiful unexpected trilling emanating from an old oak tree overhanging the garden. Looking around, I see a tiny robin has hopped into view, settled on a low, mossy branch, and is singing exquisitely and plaintively, like a choirboy, his two large black eyes fixed on my every move. For a split second, our eyes meet across the smoky ether and it feels as if the robin is performing solo, just for me, imploring me to listen to his heartfelt song. I stand and stare for a while, transfixed by the crystalline melody and as the delightful trill continues, I feel my soul lift, my senses soften and my troubled mind begin to unwind like a broken spring.

A light breeze picks up, ruffling the downy feathers on the robin's red breast and I have the urge to cradle the fragile bird in my hands. I want to stroke its tender head and its soft wings but the moment I move, it senses my advances and flits off into the dense canopy of the overhanging branches.

I continue through the gate, desperate to see my new found friend again but however hard I strain, I cannot see the robin among the tangled branches of the overhanging oak. I can still hear a faint quavering sound but, sadly, no flash of red or tell-tale movement. Instead, an unexpected memory glides across my mind. I see my father on the terrace of my childhood home in Kent chatting away to a friendly robin (as he often used to do), scattering breadcrumbs under the wooden bird table. I'm watching him from the kitchen window, munching my buttered toast before school, and straining to hear what he's saying. As usual, it involves the weather: 'It's going to be another hot day, my friend. Less chance of a nice, juicy worm; look, I've got you some suet and some bread for breakfast. You'll like that.'

My father, it seemed, was happiest in these moments.

The flashback reminds me that I haven't fed our birds for years. No wonder they've all abandoned the garden. What happened to that spanking new wooden bird table my father gave me when we moved to Oxfordshire? It must have rotted away like everything else and I didn't replace it, too busy doing other things.

After the walk, I return to the house and the first thing I do is grab a notepad and pen and start drawing up a list of things to buy for the garden birds. A feeding table is top of my list, a bird bath is next and then peanuts, sunflower seeds and suet balls. Afterwards, I head to the study where Ed and I keep our collection of family photograph albums. I want to see if there are any images of our garden in the early days before we took the weedkiller and mower to it.

The first photo I come across is of Olivia dressed in a vivid pink tutu and Sam in an oversized pirate's outfit, complete with tricorn hat and skull and crossbones. They both look adorable and appear to be standing on top of an unwieldy hillock of long grass near the oak, the same oak where I just saw the robin. I had forgotten about the "mound" as we called it back in the early days. Despite being covered in nettles and infested with rabbits, it was the kids' secret play area and they were rightly furious when Ed and I decided to remove it. I remember Sam glaring up at me from under his cap, screaming: 'You're a rabbit murderer, Mummy, you've killed our bunnies and taken away our den and now there's nowhere for us to play.'

Further on I find another image of the children, this time with my father – their Grandpa Tim. All three are beaming from ear to ear and, judging by the overflowing watering cans in their hands, they've been working together on reviving the summer wilt. He gave them both a set of gardening equipment as a house-warming present and taught them how to dig out resistant weeds with the fork and use the miniature rake to collect up autumn leaves. He even brought over two metal wheelbarrows that Simon and I used to enjoy at about the same age. I remember competing with my brother for the fullest barrow of sticks, fir cones and leaves, and chasing him around the garden, laughing hysterically as the wind whipped debris into our faces. I always made sure I won the competition.

Behind the happy trio is a large, diamond-shaped wooden trellis covered in what appears to be a spectacularly lavish and sprawling pink rose. In those days, our cottage garden was a mass of English roses – rambling, climbing, wild, shrub; you name it, we had it! They grew in abundance in the back and front garden, up the side of the house and in the borders, and the wildlife clearly loved them. The pretty, scented flowers were always a mass of butterflies and bees.

Bushy and overgrown with tall, sculptural foxgloves, weeping honeysuckle and buttery evening primrose, the trellis epitomised our eclectic jungle, but we removed it of course, along with the rambling roses and most of the shrubs in our garden. The photo is proof of that, painfully reminiscent of what we destroyed.

Behind the trellis, hidden in the long grass, I can just make out the dark shadows of the tall irises surrounding the old pond. It had its challenges in the early days – not least from a safety point of view – but the children loved our mucky mire and it seemed the more rancid and boggier it became, the happier they were. Life was never boring when fishing for tadpoles or hunting toads and newts and barely a summer's day went by when we weren't treated to an influx of damselflies or dragonflies or even an impressive acrobatic display by a squadron of swallows, eager to quench their thirst in the pooled rainwater.

As for our neatly mown lawn, the garden didn't have one back then, certainly nothing as manicured and formal as the one we have today. The previous owners – both in their eighties – had clearly stopped mowing years before we arrived and the grass had metamorphosed into an entangled meadow. Among the daisies, sedge, buttercups and dandelions grew orchids, dead-nettle, clover, toadflax and scabious, and there was always insect sound emanating from the dense pasture. The first thing Ed and I did when we arrived was scorch the wildflowers with herbicide and then raze the whole area with a new nifty sit-on mower. I blanch just thinking about it.

Feeling nostalgic and still a little sad, I close the albums and go through to the kitchen to make myself another cup of coffee. On the sideboard I spot my new wildlife gardening book which was a gift from my mother on the second anniversary of my father's death. Although she never shared his passion for nature, she knew how much it meant to Dad and how he would have sacrificed anything to see me return to my roots and resurrect my zest for wildlife. 'You can't put it off forever,' she had said warmly, 'we may not have agreed on many things – your father and I – but he was always true to himself and I loved that about him. I used to love that about you too, Annabel – your passion for nature and stubborn resistance to change. Remember what I've always said – you are your father's daughter and always will be.'

I open the book for the first time and start flicking through the chapters. Each one is beautifully illustrated with tantalising examples of gardens, both large and small, that have been successfully returned to nature. There's a chapter on birds, wildlife corridors and insect habitats and instructions on how to install the perfect pond and create a wildflower meadow full of pollinating insects, reptiles and small mammals. There's even a section on what trees, hedges, shrubs and flowers to plant to attract a rich diversity of wildlife into the garden whilst keeping it stylish and easy to maintain. To my shame, the book clearly trumpets everything I've been resisting in my own patch these past twenty years, while at the same time encompassing the very essence of what my father strove for all those many moons ago. Each of the gardens featured in the book could be my childhood garden – my father's wildlife sanctuary – and I feel, staring at the pictures, as if I'm stuck in a time warp.

I take my coffee through to the sitting room and Georgie follows. She jumps up onto the sofa beside me and snuggles down, stretching out her gangly frame and resting her warm black nose on my knee. Outside, the bright morning sunlight has sunk behind the clouds and the sky has turned an ominous slate grey, heralding a downpour. As the first heavy marbles of rain fall and ricochet off the patio stones, I lean down and whisper into Georgie's ear:

'It's redemption time, Georgie, my cue to make amends,' but she's already fallen fast asleep.

THREE

1977 – RAKES AND ADDERS

I was twelve years old when my godmother, Aunt Sue, gave me a journal for Christmas. She had drawn a pretty, white and fawn-dappled roe deer on the front cover and bound together the pages – one for every week of the year – with a silky pink ribbon. The simple diary came with a pack of five small crayons and a sophisticated, smart new fountain pen and blue ink.

I was thrilled with my present, itching to fill the empty white pages with my life's story, but when I eventually sat down at my desk to write, however hard I tried, I found my imagination deserted me and my mind went blank. I wasn't even sure how to start.

It was my father who suggested I keep a nature journal. We were outside in the garden one afternoon in the no-man's land between Christmas and New Year building a snowman and admiring the overnight transformation of the trees into crystal snow sculptures, when he said:

'You love nature; the diary could be your account of all the animals, birds and insects you discover in our secret sanctuary here.'

'But nobody would want to read that,' I retorted forlornly, 'that's a terrible idea. It's hardly Anne Frank.'

I saw a broad smile spread across his rosy cheeks. 'But think about the adventures you have with our wild animals, and even the insects you discover can be exciting and dangerous sometimes.'

'I suppose so,' I replied, unconvinced, scrunching my forehead as I tried to weigh up my father's words. He was probably right though. The garden was a treasure trove of wild creatures and I was constantly amazed by what I saw and found, like the first time I spotted a hedgehog in the long grass. It was that mellow hour before sunset and I was sitting on our wooden bench with a cup of hot chocolate before bed. It was just me in the garden, the faint scent of honeysuckle and the dying embers of sunlight. The tiny dappled hedgehog appeared first at the edge of the damp grass, twitching its pointy snout and nervously sniffing the air. It then moved surreptitiously across the lawn, oblivious to my presence, silently digging for small slugs and snails. That night, I put out a saucer of water for my new prickly friend and a bowl of crushed dog biscuits, and by morning the food had all but disappeared. I saw the hedgehog again the next night and for several nights after that until my mother banned me from putting out any more dog food and the urchin found a new home.

Later that summer, Gazelle, our elderly black Labrador, chanced upon a large, coiled adder sunning itself on a steep, grassy bank by the Victorian greenhouse. I will never forget the furore that followed. Alerted to the snake by her frantic barking, I rushed outside to find my mother wedged halfway up a tall elm tree by the greenhouse, her expensive floral dress billowing out of the dense foliage like a trapped balloon. She was hollering at my father and when Dad eventually arrived on the scene carrying a fierce garden rake, the serpent had slithered back into its hole and my mother was beside herself with anger:

'This is not the African bush, Timmy, and you're not David fucking Attenborough!' she screamed at the top of her shrill voice as Dad attempted to extract her from the tree. 'If you don't get rid of that bloody snake, I will shoot it myself with your wretched air rifle!'

Now that was a story worth recounting in my diary, I thought, chuckling to myself.

Dad often referred to our garden as a wildlife sanctuary; it certainly had a very different look to my friends' neat and tidy plots. I loved the fact it was unkempt and filled with adders and hedgehogs and that every shapeless nook and cranny was a rich mass of rainbow colours, emitting potent and tantalising scents. There was only one formal area – my mother's side of the sun terrace – where we would sit out on loungers in the summer – but otherwise, the garden was pure, untamed jungle.

'Let me show you something when we get back in the house,' my father said, stacking the wheelbarrow with the last of the winter logs. It was beginning to feel really cold outside and icicles the size of daggers had formed on the garage roof. I was looking forward to going in for a warm tea.

As we passed the open garage my father stopped in his tracks. I saw he was staring at something at the back of the lean-to. I followed his gaze and there, hidden in the straw behind a pile of wood, was a large russet fox. It had a particularly long, pointy muzzle, rimmed with downy white fur, and was staring furtively through two magnetic, amber eyes that pierced the shadowy light like oval jewels. We both froze and I felt a ripple of excitement as if someone had just handed me a new puppy. Peering up, I saw the same expression of awe on my father's face. When I glanced back, the red fox had gone, escaped through a small aperture at the back of the garage. All I saw was the tip of its white fur tail slipping silently out of sight.

'I'm sure he will return,' my father said, sensing my disquiet, 'once you are tucked up in bed. Foxes like to hunt at night, but the warm straw will tempt him back, you wait, when the cold frost starts to bite. Look out for footprints in the snow tomorrow morning.'

Mum had tea ready when we got inside. After shaking the snow off from our clothes and warming our hands by the fire, we sat down to enjoy hot toasted crumpets with melted butter and blackberry jam – a Sunday afternoon tradition. I leant back against my father's knees and stared into the red, smoky embers, dreaming of the amber-red fox and wondering where he was hiding out now.

After tea, Dad went upstairs and I heard him rummaging around in the tall bookcase on the landing. He loved books; like me, he was a rapacious reader and ever since I can remember had crammed the house from top to bottom with bookcases and shelves of all shapes and sizes. There was even an Edwardian bookcase in the tiny washroom by the front door filled with 'suitable books to pass the time when you are doing your ablutions,' my mother explained to me one day when I asked why it was there. She then added with a wry smile: 'I'm afraid your father can't survive a single moment of the day without a book. He needs one apparently even when he's on the loo!'

Dad collected books as eagerly as I collected miniature Whimsy animals and Snoopy teddies. His favourites were about nature and gardening, but he also relished anything to do with sport and military history and had an entire bookcase dedicated to African and Asian battles. He loved showing me his collection and I often thought if he hadn't become a stockbroker, he would have made the perfect librarian.

The bookcase on the landing stretched to the ceiling. It was stacked with hardback nature manuals, and some were quite old and precious and illustrated with beautiful life-size drawings. I particularly liked his collection of bird and butterfly guides – over thirty different manuals – and his miniature set of Observer's books that helped would-be naturalists like myself identify different species of insects, animals, birds, wildflowers, pondlife and trees. I often slipped them into my pocket on my daily excursions around the garden in search of new, natural treasures. On rainy days, I would sit on the landing with my legs crossed, poring over the illustrations, sapping up as much information as my curious mind could infuse.

'Have a look at this,' Dad said as he came back into the room, handing me a book I had never seen before. It had the intriguing title, *The Country Diary of an Edwardian Lady*, and a glossy cover, beautifully painted with songbirds and scarlet poppies. Inside, I saw the author, Edith Holden, had handwritten her entries using a traditional fountain pen and decorated each with an exquisite drawing, creating a captivating, detailed record of all the different wildlife she encountered on her walks through the fields, footpaths and meadows of rural Warwickshire.

I was thrilled.

'Wow,' I said, staring at a stunning picture of an electric-green and red woodpecker. 'It's beautiful, thank you.'

'You can keep it if you like; it was a Christmas gift from Granny Lagden and I was going to give it to you one day. I just needed the right opportunity. Look after it though, it's a first edition so really quite special.'

I was lost for words and simply wrapped my arms around his wide back.

'Perhaps you could do something similar,' he added as he stroked my hair and we both stared into the fire.

'I will,' I said, slowly finding my voice, 'I definitely will,' and just as our grandfather clock in the hall struck the hour, I rushed upstairs to find Aunt Sue's journal.

FOUR

THE GOOD NEIGHBOUR

I'm sitting with Ed one evening discussing ideas for a new nature garden when he suggests I ask Ron, our octogenarian neighbour, to advise on where to start. Ron has always been a keen gardener and, despite his venerable age, is rarely seen without his large digging fork which he uses for pretty much every garden job. Come rain or shine, we see him outdoors hoeing or weeding his vegetables, maintaining his extensive flowerbeds or chopping wood for his log burner under cover of the garage.

Sam and Olivia still refer to him affectionately as Worzel Gummidge due to his striking resemblance to the fantasy scarecrow, and it's not hard to see why. He's almost always clothed in the same threadbare moleskin jacket, tied at the waist with a straggly piece of tough garden yarn, and a pair of equally raggedy brown corduroy trousers that billow out from under his socks like potato sacks. His large feet are hidden in battle-hardened army boots, while his balding pate is cocooned in a mud-splattered cotton sunhat which has seen better days but effectively protects him from all manner of gardening hazards and extreme weather.

Fortunately for Ed and me, Ron's a very friendly and knowledgeable scarecrow and in the absence of my father, the first port of call if we ever need help in the garden.

'Could we buy Worzel some new trousers for Christmas, Mummy?' Sam asked a few years after we moved to our cottage. 'I'm sure his ones will need a wash soon.'

'Well, a hat would be a good idea but trousers might be pushing it,' I replied, holding back a smile.

Sam looked quizzical and scrunched his eyes.

'Well, we all have different sized bums,' I said quickly, keen to clarify. 'You might have to ask Ron his waist size and that might be a bit embarrassing.'

'I know that!' Sam snapped back defiantly, his cheeks reddening.

He shot me one of his long stern stares then and his eyes moved slowly down towards my voluminous waistline. He had noticed that a roll of lard had escaped, like a lava flow, over the top of my buttonless jeans. I waited, with bated breath, for the inevitable put-down.

'Your bum is absolutely enormous!' he gushed finally, throwing back his blond locks in mock-horror and giggling hysterically before rushing out of the door.

When it came to compiling his stocking list a few weeks later, Sam asked Father Christmas for a new cotton sunhat to fit "an old man like you" and a pair of woolly "grandpa" socks to fit a "giant scarecrow". On Christmas morning, his eyes lit up like flares when he discovered the two items tucked at the bottom of his stocking, neatly wrapped and bearing a special Father Christmas tag – *For Ron* – and Ron's eyes lit up like baubles when he received the unexpected gifts. A basket of freshly baked rolls appeared outside our front door the very next day as a token of his thanks.

These days, Ron tips Sam's floppy sunhat whenever he sees me across the garden fence and we often chat about the children or the weather. His angular, heavily lined face carries a perceptible world-weariness, but when he smiles, his large eyes still dance and sparkle, and his cheeks redden and swell like two round pippins.

He lives alone and has done ever since his wife passed away within a week of us moving in, but he seems contented enough. His one regular visitor is his daughter, Julia, who comes to help him in the garden and check he has enough firewood and food. I've often tried inviting him over for a cup of tea but he politely refuses, preferring instead to chat over the garden gate.

Today, however, he's broken a twenty-year-old tradition and accepted my invitation to tea and chocolate cake on the terrace. I grab some old wooden deck chairs and we sit facing the late-afternoon sun, which is still gloriously aglow across both our gardens. I can see the maroon leaves of his copper beech protruding over the top of the dividing hedge and notice a loud humming coming from the tree.

'That's the ivy, my dear,' he says, picking up on my thoughts. 'The bees love the berries at this time of year.'

'Do they?' I reply, amazed. 'I always thought ivy was considered a menace. I've been pulling it out for years.'

'You don't want to do that, dear, not the native variety, hedera helix – that won't harm anything, and the butterflies, moths and birds will love it too, particularly the flowers. You want to encourage it to grow, if you can.'

I hand him his tea and we chat for a while about the children and Ed's new teaching job. He's always been interested in the family. When I tell him that both Sam and Olivia are almost finished school, he laughs.

'I can't believe that, dear. Doesn't seem like yesterday that they were as small as one of those flowerpots over there and playing in the garden.'

He points to a set of miniature flower pots by the kitchen window and winks, playfully.

I think back warmly to those halcyon childhood days and remember how sweet Ron was with the kids. He often played peekaboo through the beech hedge or pulled funny faces when they rushed to greet him at the gate and I would stand at the kitchen sink listening, captivated by the cackle of giggles and whoops of surprise that echoed joyfully through the garden. Occasionally, he would leave a carton of home-grown vegetables by the front door with a sticky label attached saying, *For your dinner* or *Not to be eaten raw!* I remember Olivia rushing into the kitchen once with her pockets overflowing with fresh potatoes and green beans, screaming: 'Look what Worzel Gummidge has given us. Can we have them for tea, Mummy, please?'

On another occasion, he came to the front door carrying an extremely long ladder to inform me that one of Olivia's school friends was stuck in a tree at the end of the garden and he was heading down to help. In the time it took me to find a pair of wellington boots, put the door on the latch and charge to the offending tree, Ron had expertly coaxed the frightened girl down from her precarious perch and wrapped her in his threadbare jacket. I was so relieved; I could have hugged him.

He never asked for anything in return for his neighbourly kindnesses other than the occasional chat over the garden fence, and the only time he sought my help was when his daughter was away on holiday and he had run out of flour for his lunchtime rolls. He baked all his own bread but, despite there being a supermarket in the next-door village, he insisted on making a two-hour round trip by car to a local mill where he could buy a freshly milled sack of organic flour. One bag, he boasted, would keep him in bread rolls for a whole month. I didn't mind the journey; it gave me an opportunity, finally, to repay him for his many favours.

He was surprisingly chatty in the car, eager to tell me all about his garden, his career as a chef in Wales and his youngest son who had passed away, tragically. It was the first time I remember him opening up to me and I was content to listen and get to know the man I had shared just fleeting conversations with over the years. He clearly loved nature and wildlife gardening and fervently believed we should all be self-sufficient and, at the very least, grow our own vegetables.

'All of us men should be like Tom and you ladies like Barbara in *The Good Life*, dear,' he chortled from under his cotton cap. 'There's nothing better than home-grown fruit and veg. It tastes better, cooks better and it doesn't harm the environment – beats the supermarket stuff any day.'

After our trip, the next morning, he left a hefty carton of ruby-red wild strawberries outside our front door, fresh from his garden and with a note attached saying: *Thank you, my dear, for listening to an old man and for the lift.*

The shadows in the garden are lengthening, and Ron sits silently staring out at my bland flowerbeds and huge lawn. He has a whimsical expression and, knowing how much he cares for natural gardens and wild spaces, I imagine he's wholeheartedly disappointed by what he sees.

'You must hate the way the garden looks,' I say apologetically, breaking the silence and feeling my cheeks slowly redden. 'I know my father would be disappointed, if he were here. I so wish we hadn't ripped everything out – the pond, the trees, the wildflowers and the long grass. We wouldn't have lost the wildlife, I'm sure of it.'

Ron turns to face me, and I can see his expression has softened. I continue, my shame abating, slightly.

'I know how busy you are, I've seen you in your garden, but I was wondering, hoping perhaps you might help me with mine. I want to rewild it, you see, but I need someone to guide me, someone knowledgeable like you. Do you think you could help? Guide me that is?'

I pause for a moment, fearing that my show of emotion might be too much for Ron, so used to his privacy, but he seems unfazed and, more to the point, is still smiling. Leaning forwards, he pats me gently on the back and, speaking softly, says: 'Of course, my dear, I would be delighted to help. We all get it wrong sometimes. No point in fretting. The garden will come back. That's the beauty of nature. It has a wonderful capacity to regenerate itself, and it will change overnight if you get the balance right.'

I feel relief course through me and then pressure suddenly and unexpectedly building behind my eyes. His kindness is almost overwhelming, and I find myself struggling to hold back tears. 'I do hope so, Ron, I really do. The thing is, I'm not sure I can do it alone and not having Dad anymore, well I don't know who else to ask.'

He's visibly moved and I can see his apple cheeks have gone a shade darker. Tiny droplets of sweat cling to his brow and as he wipes them away with a large spotty handkerchief, he turns to me and smiles: 'Your father was a true naturalist and a great gardener. I used to watch him with Sam and Olivia here before he died. I'm sure you miss him, but he would understand. Don't beat yourself up over it.'

I look away as tears pour down my cheeks.

'Come with me, Annabel – I want to show you something,' he says, quickly brightening up. I wipe my eyes with the back of my hand and he heaves himself out of the low wooden chair, stretching his hunched shoulders.

Intrigued, I accompany him through the gate, wondering what he has in store, and we walk slowly down into his long, narrow garden, passing crescent-shaped borders graced with herbs, heather, faded lavender and a host of stunning purple and red salvias. Eventually, we reach a wooden bench cocooned within a circle of silver birch and he invites me to sit down next to him. Through the mottled, bone whistle trunks of the birch, I can see the entirety of his sun-kissed garden, and it appears mystical and soft in the dying embers of light.

'Do you remember what this garden looked like in the early days, when you first moved in next door? It used to be mainly lawn and formal flowerbeds. Well, I let it all go a few years ago and, well, what do you think?'

My first impression is disbelief; the garden looks so different. The neat contours of the flowerbeds have entirely disappeared and the shrubs and cultivated plants that I remember have been subsumed by wildflowers, creepers and long flowing grass. It's as if nature has taken over and produced its own unique hue and shape. But what's most striking about the change is the abundance of life amid the vegetation. There are dozens of different pollinators – wasps, bees, butterflies, moths, hoverflies, even a tiger-toned dragonfly – all eagerly searching for their share of late-summer nectar and, tucked away within the dense shrubbery, I can see warblers, tits, finches and robins flitting from stem to stem, enjoying the security of the foliage.

'This is gorgeous,' I say, brimming over with envy, 'I had no idea you had done this to your garden.'

Ron slowly gets up and I follow him further into his wildlife haven. I feel strangely like my father's lapdog again, the adult version, and full of curiosity to know all about the flora and fauna in the garden. I want the names of the insects flying around the plants, the birds flitting from branch to branch and the scents I can smell, but, despite my new-found verve, I resist the temptation to bombard Ron with questions.

We reach the southern end of his garden by the cemetery, once a dull patch of scrub and grass but now a meadow of cowslip, daisy, wild marjoram, clover, self-heal and cow parsley. As we get closer, I can hear a low humming sound and notice it's swarming with more pollinating insects.

I gasp. 'I really can't believe what you've done here, Ron! It's so vibrant. How did you do it?'

'I did nothing, my dear, at least for the first few years. If you want to get wildlife back into your garden, you just need to stop gardening; plant a few native wildflowers to get you started and then let nature do the rest.'

I return to the house flushed with hope and enthusiasm. If Ron's garden can be transformed in just a few years, there is still hope for mine.

I spend a fruitful evening immersed in my new wildlife guide, surrounded by my father's old gardening books, drawing diagrams and making a few rough notes. The next morning, I wake to find a mysterious, handwritten note on the doormat outside my front door. It's a list of wildlife-friendly plants that Ron has compiled for me overnight; varieties he recommends for our chalky soil that will create all-year-round colour and scent. He's even drawn a diagram suggesting where I should plant them.

At the bottom of the list is a quote from AA Milne's *Winnie the Pooh*: *Weeds are flowers too, once you get to know them*, and underneath that he's drawn a smiley face and added a postscript: *Be patient, Annabel. Rome wasn't built in a day – be prepared to lose a bit along the way.*

I dash over to thank him but he's already out in his garden, busy tending to his vegetable patch. I leave him in peace. Now that I have his list, I have somewhere to start; I return inside and start properly designing my new wildlife garden.

FIVE

BIRDS OF A FEATHER

We moved to the Old Coach House, my childhood home, in 1967 when my brother was four and I was nearly three and my only recollection from that time, apart from the mystery and magic of the wild garden, was its penetrating cold and damp and the vast emptiness of the place. With its imposing black and white façade and lofty position at the pinnacle of a steep hill, the house reminded me of one of the mystical fairy tale castles in the stories my father read to me before bedtime.

Built in the eighteenth century for horses and carriages belonging to the local Manor, our home had never been intended as a warm, family residence and required a mountain of work in the early days to make it even vaguely habitable. There was no central heating and minimal insulation, forcing my father to employ a friendly, local builder to install a large brick fireplace in the biggest room in the house – the carriage room – which was also the coldest room on account of it having six vast, single-paned windows. Poorly constructed,

28

the lopsided chimney billowed out clouds of sooty smoke whenever the fire was lit, which resulted in my father having to quickly open all the vast windows, leading to an artic gale swirling through the house. After some Herculean stoking, the fire would eventually take hold and my father would nip round the room with a duster, which he kept hidden in a secret drawer, frantically cleaning my mother's precious porcelain and valuable paintings before they succumbed to a thick layer of harmful coal dust, and we all succumbed to her ire.

It wasn't uncommon, in the heart of winter, for Jack Frost to leave a white curtain of ice on the inside of our bedroom windows in the morning, and I would often lie in bed watching the Indian smoke rings of my breath slowly rise to the ceiling, putting off the dreaded moment when I would have to make a dash for the bathroom. On really cold nights – and winters were blistering at times in the 1970s – I would sneak through to my brother's bedroom, wrapped in my heavy wool blanket, and snuggle down next to him. With our legs and arms curled around each other, we were like a pair of hibernating badger cubs.

After finally installing radiators, Dad refused to have them on for more than three hours a day, even when the mercury in our outdoor thermometer dipped below zero and the water in the taps froze. 'It's your father's natural abstemiousness,' my mother remarked one particularly freezing afternoon before Christmas. 'It stems from the war years, I'm afraid, and having to go without the normal comforts. Heating was a luxury then.' My brother and I weren't convinced. We thought Dad was just being mean. 'Toughen you up a bit,' he would say in his best sergeant major voice as we stood in our bedrooms after our twice-weekly tepid bath shivering like clockwork mice in a small towel.

There were upsides, though, to the cold, and most winter evenings Dad would sit with me by the fire and we would either flick through one of his nature books or he would tell me a story. I loved his stories; it seemed the more he told, the more far-fetched they became, absorbing me deeper and deeper into his fantasy world of wildlife and magic. He often invented fantastical tales about the house and our wildlife garden and sometimes they were entangled, like the one about the bronze cockerel weathervane on the roof that loomed over us like a majestic figurehead on the prow of a ship. 'Let me tell you about our magical cockerel,' he said one evening as we sat by the log fire listening to the wind howling in the rafters. I had snuggled down into the warm folds of his thick, Jacob's sheep jumper to keep warm.

'When it's sunny and hot, the cockerel spins round to face south and sings a happy tune. You might have heard it.' My father then attempted a rather feeble cock-a-doodle-do impression, making me giggle. 'But when it's cold and windy, like it is tonight, the cockerel swings to the north and falls silent. He hates storms, you see, just like you, but he's patient and knows that after every tempest, the sun will rise again.'

Later, when I was older and learning geography and science for the first time, he used the bronze weathervane to explain to me the importance of our seasons in the cycle of life. I still have his explanation written down in my nature diary:

Every living thing on earth is reliant on the changing seasons. Spring brings courtship, nesting and new life, summer brings warmth and an abundance of food for our wild creatures, autumn sounds a clarion call for migration and hibernation while the cold of winter is vital for germination and rebirth. Just like us, nature needs the changing seasons to navigate life; tip the balance and the natural lifecycle falls apart.

One of Dad's great passions was birdwatching, and I would often see him at the kitchen window adjusting his old field glasses before focusing them on the wooden bird table. The glasses were a relic from his two years of National Service in Kenya, but they still worked, just, despite the lenses being impractically small.

'Just seen a beautiful pair of bullfinches hoovering up the crumbs I left earlier,' he said one morning as I shuffled into the kitchen, late for my breakfast. It was a Sunday; my mother was fast asleep still (she always had a lie-in at the weekend) and my brother was away at boarding school; it was just me and Dad, together in our special time. He had cooked bacon and eggs and the smell had permeated up through the kitchen ceiling into my bedroom above. I sat down at the bar table with my plate of food and a cup of cold milk and stared out at the terrace, straining to see through the film of condensation that was streaming down the glass like the Niagara Falls. It was mid-February and still cold outside.

'They are handsome creatures, but they're devils with fruit blossom,' he said, with his glasses still fixed on the pink-chested finches. 'There, look, behind the rose, you can just see the female; she's paler than the male, less vibrant but just as grand.'

I noticed that the bird table was already topped up with yesterday's leftover pork crackling, and Dad had even skewered a large wedge of stale bread to a nail sticking up from the wooden roof, hoping, no doubt, his feathered friends might finish it off for him. He would try anything to avoid waste!

We counted twelve different species visiting the bird table that morning including a chaffinch, a blackcap, a siskin (seen enjoying the peanuts), a nuthatch and numerous hedge and house sparrows.

Later, after breakfast, I was staring out of the bathroom window watching Dad ferreting around by our old Victorian well when I saw him turn and stare at the wall below my window. Something had attracted his attention. He started beckoning to me, so I quickly finished what I was doing and charged downstairs, eager to join in his discovery. Treading gently to dim the crunching sound of frost underfoot, I crept slowly across the hardened grass until I reached my father. At first, I couldn't see anything except the back wall of the house but then, as I focused my eye more sharply, I saw four or maybe five magnificent birds perched on the sprawling cotoneaster plant. They were gorging on the red berries, seemingly oblivious to our presence. Despite being several feet away, I could see red, black and white streaks on their elegant wings, and there were bright yellow spots on the wing tips. Their lofty heads were adorned with exotic native Indian-style head feathers and they were unlike any bird I had ever seen before, even in my father's nature books.

'What are they, Dad? They're amazing.'

'Waxwings, Annabel, and they don't normally come this far west; they usually migrate to central Europe in winter and then nest in Scandinavia in summer. Beats a house sparrow any day, don't you agree?'

I was awestruck.

SIX
NESTING INSTINCT

I've bought a wooden bird box which I want to erect in a quiet part of the garden, as recommended by my wildlife book, and I've asked Ron over to help. After our tea on the terrace, he's been particularly attentive and keen to offer me words of wisdom and encouragement whenever he catches me at the gate. He arrives with his long ladder and we amble down to a tall larch where I've chosen to site the box.

'You could plant at least thirty tree saplings in this space,' he says as we reach the larch. He's pointing to a bare stretch of manicured lawn, about the size of a tennis court, stretching from our drive to the main road.

'I was hoping we could plant some Ron, but I didn't think we had room for that many!'

'You'd be surprised, my dear. The most important thing is having light and free-draining soil, and you've got both here.'

He leans the ladder against the ridged trunk of the larch and clambers awkwardly up, clutching the box in one hand and his tools in the other. I can barely watch. He's less agile than he used to be, and his floppy hat and voluminous trousers are flapping badly in the wind. 'Be careful!' I shout up, but he's forgotten to turn up his hearing aid and my plea falls on deaf ears. At one point, he loses his balance and several screws come clattering down the ladder like coins. They disappear into the grass as I push my knee more firmly into the bottom rung.

It takes him several attempts to get the bird box straight but eventually he fixes it and I let out a huge sigh of relief when a pair of cracked boots and tattered corduroys appear again on the ground.

'Would you mind if I take a quick peep inside the box?' I say after he's wiped his brow and removed the larch needles from his hat. 'I've got some straw to put in the box to make it cosy and warm for the birds.'

'Of course, dear, but watch out, the ladder's unsteady.'

'I know!' I say nervously, starting my ascent. 'I haven't climbed a tree since I was a young girl.'

The sensation of the climb combined with the excitement of being close to trees again transports me, in an eye blink, back to my childhood, to lazy afternoons spent scaling tall trees, playing pirates from my tree house and swinging chimpanzee-style from a low sturdy branch. Loving the gush of energy and brush of my ponytail against the long, swaying grass, I remember how the excitement of the swing made me holler and scream; so much so that my poor mother would be forced to drop what she was doing and rush to my assistance. How fearless I was then, I think now, how unrestrained by rules and regulations and how wonderful it feels to be back climbing a tree, if just to peep inside a tiny bird box.

Simon and I would stay in the fruit trees until the sun sank below the valley and the night sky turned into a planetarium. We would pretend we were pirates or astronauts then and spy on Mum and Dad as they pottered around the house, and we would laugh as we dropped twigs and fruit on Gazelle as she sat patiently on the ground below, her ears pricked, waiting for us to come down and take her inside.

As Ron holds the ladder, I clamber down through the pendulous canopy of needles and branches, stroking the scaly bark and drawing in its rich, spicy aroma – a combination of musk, resin and sap. I can see right across the top of the garden from my mid-way position to the lower end by the cemetery and notice the neat grass is still basked in sunlight, even at this late hour. It occurs to me, suddenly, that the spot would make the perfect location for a wildflower meadow – flat and sunny and far enough from trees to avoid getting coated in leaves. Presumably, the clover, scabious, oxeye daisies and all the other pretty wildflowers that once grew at the bottom of our garden, would still be there lying dormant under the finely cut lawn.

Looking in the opposite direction through the sun-dappled trees, I glimpse the wooded top of the North Wessex Downs. Up until the mid-nineteenth century, this whole area would have been a dense forest of beech, ash, elm, willow, hazel and oak and inhabited, not by people, but by deer, foxes, badgers, nightingales, owls, woodpeckers, bats and even wild boar. Before the advent of hard machinery, the local villagers and tradesmen would have visited our hillside to coppice the trees for timber and make charcoal and firewood out of the fallen branches. They would have relied on the trees for hunting animals and the understory of scrub for foraging insects, fruits, berries and mushrooms.

Now just fragments of the original forest remain and the lank, grassy stretch below me has become a redundant space, used only occasionally for croquet or football in summer. Ron is right. It's crying out to be wooded again.

I glance once more at the garden and then complete my descent, feeling a welcome sense of satisfaction at getting the shelter up and excited at the thought that a songbird might soon discover it and turn it into a home.

I invite Ron back to the house for a cup of tea and a piece of chocolate cake. I'm definitely feeling more comfortable in his company and I'm sensing that he feels the same with me. We sit on the swing seat together, silently sipping our tea and sapping up the last of the sun's rays and I observe, with pride, that my new bird feeding station is busy attracting some new black-capped birds.

'Those are coal tits, dear,' Ron says, noticing my surprise. 'I get them my side too. Perhaps they've spotted us putting up the bird box and want to nab the first viewing. They usually nest in dead trunks and cavities but the odd one will settle for a wooden shelter.'

The monkish tits fly off, their greenish-grey backs catching the sunlight as they dart and dive. I notice the apple trees behind us are beginning to lose their leaves. Soon all the trees in the garden will be undergoing their autumn transformation and becoming skeletal and brown once again.

'When do you think I should plant the trees?' I ask eagerly, keen to get the tree planting underway as soon as possible, but Ron's eyes have closed in the sunshine and he looks on the verge of nodding off. I give the seat a gentle rock.

'What was that, dear?' he says, coming round suddenly.

I repeat the question, this time with a little more resonance.

'Ah, well, I would wait till early winter for that, my dear. The sap's dormant then and the ground is soft, which makes it easier for digging. You'll need to continue watering the saplings for at least a year or two while the roots get established.'

He takes a glug of tea and then starts on the cake, spilling crumbs down his woollen jumper. Flicking them onto the ground, he disturbs Georgie, who has been lying quietly all this time under our feet. She leaps up and knocks Ron's arm, spilling tea and cake everywhere.

'Georgie!' I scream, but it's too late, she's all over us, desperately trying to scoop up the bits like a snuffling pig.

We both move away, leaving Georgie to her feast. It's time, anyway, for Ron to return home. He wants to make his bread rolls and after retrieving his hat, which has fallen on the ground, I accompany him back to the gate, eager to extend our chat for as long as possible.

'What trees would you plant if you were me?'

'Native ones, dear, and a good mix. Add to what you've got already –
beech, oak, hazel and maybe some Scots pine. You can't go wrong if you
do that, and plant more sorbus and prunus if you like; the birds and bees
will love the fruits and berries.'

I thank him and we say our goodbyes at the gate but, before going
inside, I return to the bird box for one last look. As I shuffle my way
through the fallen leaves, I notice that the sun has dipped behind the
trees and left a rich, orange glow on the glistening grass. Peering down
to take a closer look, I catch a glimpse of a solitary pink flower. It has
striking, star-shaped petals, a long stem and small, conical leaves and I
have vague memories of seeing it in my childhood garden, but the name
escapes me. Keen to quench my curiosity, I run back to the house for
my father's *Observer's Book of Wild Flowers* which never left my side as
a young girl. Faded now and worn, this pint-sized encyclopaedia with its
dainty drawings used to be my constant guide as I wandered the fields
and footpaths around the coach house in search of new, exciting varieties
of wildflower.

The flower is a campion. We did have them in Kent all those years
ago and I remember they were renowned for their mystical qualities,
once thought to guard bees' honey stores and hide fairies. It's heartening
to find such an exquisite flower in our garden this late in the year and my
last thought before I go inside is that a passing bumblebee, moth or wasp
will hopefully discover the nectar before winter takes hold.

SEVEN

ARTEMIS

My tree house was the best vantage point to see my magical childhood garden in its entirety. It was nestled between four tall elm trees right at the top of our meadow, and if I stood up on the platform, I could see over the greenhouse to the terrace by the kitchen and across the beech hedge to Dad's vegetable patch. On clear days, I could even see as far as the Norman sandstone belltower of our village church across the valley. My father had constructed it when I was five or six so my brother and I could start climbing trees. He said it was important to smell the sap, listen to the rustling of leaves and see the world like a bird, a monkey or a squirrel. He never joined us in our den. It was our sanctity where we could escape to, scheme and play without the prying eyes of our parents. It had a sturdy wooden base and tall sides constructed from old brown Formica kitchen units, but it lacked a roof so, when the weather deteriorated, I would drape a large sheet over four tall poles fixed to the sides and create a tent-like shelter that offered some temporary relief from the rain. Directly below the treehouse was a small apple orchard and grassy meadow where Simon and I would play football and cricket in summer, swing from the branches and pick rosy-red pippin apples in autumn.

One lazy afternoon in the heart of the hot summer of 1976, I had sneaked my father's old bow and arrow set into the tree house and was devising an imaginary game of cowboys and Indians when the idea came to me that I could use Dad's shiny bald pate as a target. He was in full view, happily clipping tomatoes in his greenhouse over twenty metres away and humminng the theme tune to Jesus Christ Superstar. He had no idea I was aiming my metal-tipped arrow right at him and I had no idea, at least in the seconds before I released it from its extensive bow, that it would ever reach its intended target.

When it sliced through the thin glass roof of the plant house and showered his pots and all his precious tomatoes with hundreds of tiny shards of glass, I was horror-struck. I saw my father stagger out onto the lawn, shaking glass from his clothes with a red-hot expression etched on his face. As quick as a flash, I shimmied down the rope ladder, jumping the last few rungs onto the grass below, then shot off to hide at the top of a very tall fir tree at the bottom of the garden. I remained there, concealed in the dense tangle of branches, terrified and ashamed until the sun sank below the trees and I could hear the ominous hooting of our tawny owls, the rustling of tiny creatures returning to their night-time haunts and my mother's frantic calls beckoning me inside for supper.

My father caught me sneaking through the front door and summoned me immediately into his study. He was sitting behind his heavy mahogany desk in a high-backed leather armchair, drinking from a hefty glass of whisky and nibbling peanuts. On his desk were four tomatoes, a broken arrow and several pieces of the greenhouse roof.

'That was an unbelievably stupid thing you did today,' he said, glaring at me from behind his dark-rimmed spectacles, just like Eric Morecambe from the *Morecambe and Wise Show*.

'What on earth did you think you were doing? Trying to finish me off with my father's vintage bow and arrow?'

'I'm so sorry, Dad, it was an accident, I promise, I was only playing. I didn't know it was Grandpa's. I would never have taken it if I'd known.'

'Well, you did and you ruined my greenhouse roof in the process.' As he twiddled the broken arrow absently in his hand, I noticed he had plasters on both his thumbs.

After a lengthy pause, he continued, his mood lifting slightly. 'Well, you're a bloody lucky lady. I've had some time to dwell on this and I'm willing, probably against my better judgement, to forgive you. Your grandfather, Reggie, was a very fine archer in his day and those are his trophies from school.' I followed his gaze as he pointed, proudly, to a shelf of glistening silverware.

'You seem to have inherited his eye, my dear, and for that reason I'm not going to ban you from using his bow and arrow – the obvious course of action – I'm going to sign you up for archery lessons at school instead. That is, after you've helped me mend the blessed greenhouse!'

He called me "Artemis" after that and pinned an archery target on the garage wall for me to use. 'Practice makes perfect,' he would say enthusiastically every time we passed the garage. Unfortunately, despite many hours struggling to perfect my shot, I never won any trophies.

I'm trying out my father's national service field glasses in the garden in Oxfordshire and trying to spot birds from the kitchen window as they come to investigate my swish new feeding station. I bought the large, multi-limbed metal contraption from our local garden centre along with a resin bird bath – very different from my father's single-deck, wooden bird table with its pitched roof, but just as effective. I've had a steady stream of garden favourites since including a blue tit, great tit, several coal tits, a robin and my first pair of chaffinches. I'm proud to be catering for every conceivable avian preference offering peanut, fat ball, seed, sunflower, even mealworm, and I'm hoping my bird restaurant will tempt some of the songbirds to stay and nest here.

Earlier this week, I found two large, hardback colour guides to British birds in my father's old trunk, and I use every spare moment to dip into them and re-familiarise myself with our native birds. I'm keen to identify the different species again, distinguish between the sexes and remind myself of their traits. Do they eat seeds, berries or insects? Do they prefer nesting in trees, hedges, shrubs, dead trunks or buildings and, if they don't migrate, where do they stay in the UK?

Rediscovering the old tomes has stirred a host of hidden memories and reignited a hobby I thought I had left behind decades ago. They were a gift from my grandmother, Granny Lagden, who, like my father, adored wildlife and was particularly passionate about birds. Her small cottage in Surrey was stuffed full of pretty porcelain miniatures of garden birds – warblers, tits, sparrows, finches, blackbirds, woodpeckers, doves and thrushes – and her walls were bedecked with expensive Edwardian prints of exotic species like pheasants, waxwings and owls.

As she got older and less mobile, she would sit outside her back door, her thinning bob of silver-grey hair hanging across her grooved forehead, and chat non-stop as I weeded her front border. Sipping from a large tumbler of whisky, just like my father, she would roll up her woollen skirt above her ivory-smooth knees to catch the sun and let her thick, nylon stockings drop to her ankles. They lay in folds, like drawn curtains around her Oxford brogues as she regaled me with fascinating tales about the "little creatures" she encountered in her small but thriving wildlife garden. There was Mick, the mouse, who had taken up residence under the wisteria and would appear every day at exactly 10 a.m. to collect the breadcrumbs she had left on the terrace for him. There was Tony, the blue tit, who sang lustily from the top of the hawthorn and was always the first to swoop down when she refilled the nut feeder and there was Tiddler, the toad, who lived in a shallow burrow by the pond. Tiddler had a huge sexual appetite and, seemingly being the only male toad in the garden, spent what seemed like an entire mating season copulating with every local female, his eager arms permanently bound around their sticky bodies. 'A bit like your grandfather when he was a young man,' my grandmother would snort out loud, spilling her whisky and making me blush with embarrassment.

These were memorable times for me, stoking my burgeoning fascination for wildlife and giving me a wonderful insight into my grandmother's eccentric, Victorian world. As I beavered away in her flower beds, happily chatting to her while she drank whisky and fed cheesy biscuits to her obese miniature Schnauzer, I was treated to a unique and colourful interpretation of nature alongside an unforgettable introduction to sex.

When she wasn't recounting funny stories, Granny was reminiscing about the war years and her bizarre but happy marriage to my grandfather, Reggie. Reggie was an adventurer and businessman who ran a large tea plantation in the foothills of Bengal before the outbreak of the Second World War in 1940. He had little contact with Granny during those years, apart from the odd home visit, and even less with their six children. When he did eventually make it home to Surrey, it was, mostly, 'to sire another little Lagden,' as Granny put it, flashing me one of her lobsided, cheeky grins and making me blush again.

Reggie was in India when my father, Tim, was born in the early hours of 11 January 1936 and, although delighted to have another son – he had four daughters already – he only managed to return to see his latest little Lagden a few days before my father's first birthday. After war broke out, Reggie became more and more embroiled in the Indian war effort and his home visits got fewer and fewer. Eventually, they stopped altogether.

My father was just eight years old when his prep school headmaster summoned him into his office one morning in late October 1944. He was told his father had died tragically in a plane crash while on government duty in India. There was no hug, no message from his mother, no compassionate leave and no funeral. My father was simply returned to the classroom and told to get on with it.

Sometimes when I was snuggled on his knee, listening to his heart pumping, he would tell me about that fateful day.

'I didn't cry; can you believe it? It was as if the headmaster was talking about a stranger. I hardly knew my father, you see. It's hard for you to understand, but it was different in those days. Fathers weren't always around for their children and death was everywhere.'

I realise now that Dad never really came to terms with losing his father so young and spilling out his heart to me was, somehow, his way of justifying to himself his response (or lack of response) to his death. I listened intently but I was only six or seven and the grief was lost on me. To me, the tragedy was just another of my father's fascinating stories.

It seems like only yesterday that my father was here at the cottage, guiding me in the garden. He loved being of help in the early days, before we removed the wildness. I think it reminded him of my childhood. He loved the mayhem of our borders, the mass of self-seeded wildflowers and the diversity of colour and smell, and, like Ron, he always knew exactly what to do. He would work his way through the flowerbeds, clearing invasive weeds, but leaving the rest to naturalise with the shrubs and cultivated flowers; he would cut back the bramble just enough to allow for new growth; leave patches of the lawn uncut, and risk life and limb training scented roses, vines and a passionflower around the house. He would immerse himself in chores from dawn to dusk, often with the children in tow, only ever returning indoors after sunset or for a meal or cold beer.

I took his help for granted and when we eventually altered the garden, he did less and less. He never criticised Ed or me for removing the wildlife habitats, but I sensed his sadness when we were in the garden together talking about the good old days, and I didn't push him when he became too ill and eventually stopped helping altogether.

Dad's cancer was a shock to us all. My mother said he was potting plants in his greenhouse one moment and stricken with nausea and bed-bound the next. But, as with life, Dad faced his inevitable death with characteristic stoicism. In the four years he battled illness, he never lost his sense of humour or let the disease inside him cloud his wonder for the world.

I made a point of picking a bunch of flowers from his garden every time I visited him in hospital, and he always beamed from ear to ear when I walked in.

'I hope your mother didn't see you picking those, they're her prized hydrangeas,' he said with a twinkle in his eye on the last occasion I visited. He looked so helpless and skeletal that I burst into tears.

'Don't cry, Artemis.'

I held his hand at that moment and kissed his forehead and before he shut his eyes to rest, he squeezed my fingers and whispered: 'I'm not afraid to die, you know. It's the most natural thing in the world. We all have to return to the earth eventually.'

EIGHT
POPPY FIELDS
AND HAY MEADOWS

I want to be brave like Ron and let the garden rewild itself, but having spent so long fussing over neatness, I don't feel quite ready to relinquish the reins of my control. I'm also aware that, unlike Ron's magnificent, disorderly space, my own garden lacks even the basic elements for attracting wildlife. My expert guide lists these as: water provision (a pond, fountain and/or bird baths); access points to other green spaces (holes in the fences and safe corridors around the boundaries); natural wildlife habitats (homes and shelters for insects, birds, mammals and reptiles); a compost heap and an all-round supply of food for our wildlife whether in tree, shrub or plant-based form, decaying wood or bird feeders. I feel these basic components need to be installed before I can sit back and let nature take over. With this list in mind, I print out my own rewilding manifesto and pin it to the

MY WILDING MANIFESTO

free movement

- I will create "green" corridors and access points around the garden perimeter to give wildlife freedom to roam from our garden into our neighbours' gardens and into the fields beyond the cemetery.

water

- I will reinstate the garden pond and erect more bird baths to attract a diversity of wildlife back into the garden.

food

- I will recreate areas for wildflowers and mow the lawns less often to allow wildflowers to grow through the grass!
- I will revive the herbaceous borders by adding more wildlife-friendly plants that grow well in this area. (Refer to Ron's list.)
- Once established, I will allow the new shrubs and flowers to naturalise with the wild and add herbs and wildflower seed.
- I will plant a new woodland, restore the hedgerows and increase the number of fruit and berry trees in the orchard.
- I will leave the branches and trunks of trees to rot down naturally instead of chucking them on the bonfire and create (or at least try to create) insect hotels, bee hotels and homes for hedgehogs!

protection

- I will resist the temptation to clear the garden of ivy, bramble, thistle, nettle or holly, however much my mother tries to make me.
- I will let dead trees and rotten branches die down naturally, however unsightly they may be, and will never ever cut down another mature tree again, unless it's diseased or unsafe. Even then, I will leave the base of the trunk for insects and birds to enjoy.
- I will create a natural log pile for insects, birds and small creatures and an organic home compost heap.
- I will stop using peat-based fertiliser, pesticides, slug and snail pellets and weedkiller *immediately.*

fridge door where I will see it often; it will act as my daily reminder of the tasks that lie ahead.

Later, I take a notepad around the garden with Georgie to mark up where I want to position the new wildlife features. A cool October breeze is rustling the leaves and I am just about to turn back to the house when a couple of large rooks appear overhead, zigzagging across the sky. It feels like a personal fly-past but there's something menacing about their presence too. Perhaps they know something I don't. Their grating caw slowly fades as they disappear from view.

It was still fashionable to collect and press wildflowers when I was growing up, as it was to make daisy chains and play the dandelion clock game. Knowing the names of wildflowers was as important then as knowing your times tables and every summer term, without fail, our teacher would take us on a class nature trail so we could learn more about them.

Some of the first wildflowers I ever saw were in and around the terrace my father built for the family soon after we moved to the coach house. Constructed on a slope, the garden was not ideal for a patio, but Dad hired a local builder to level out the stony escarpment and then created vertical flowerbeds from the steep earthy sides. We all helped to build a low wall round the terrace with an eclectic mix of old bricks, stone and glass bottles. I enjoyed designing the borders with my mother. Together, we planted ornamental trees, shrubs and plants that, in time, grew into a curtain of sweet-scented coloured shapes and patterns. My mother adopted one half of the terrace and my father the other. My mother's side was neat and tidy and contained mainly foreign maples, azaleas and camellias in rich, vibrant colours, while my father chose the cheaper option of sowing seed rather than buying well-established plants and using cuttings from his greenhouse. While my mother's garden exuded exoticism and sophistication with its heady mix of reds, pinks and magenta, my father's offered a pastel contrast and a natural English simplicity which was both charming and pretty.

They were at their best in late spring and summer when the butterflies would descend on the nectar-filled azaleas and camellias and the bees would swarm around Dad's foxgloves and St John's wort, serenading us as we sat on the terrace having lunch with friends or snoozed on loungers in the hot sun.

As the years went by, the wildflowers spread on the patio until even my mother's cultivated side began to look wild and unkempt. I loved the way the terrace was a revolving wheel of new species and found I was never short of things to record later in my nature diary. I found harebells, campions, orchids, scabious and primroses and then one spring, I found the terrace had been transformed into a blue carpet of sweet violet. The tiny flowers had naturalised everywhere and the honey aroma that filled the air was more beautiful and potent than any of my mother's expensive perfumes.

'All our gardens are sleeping meadows,' my father said to me one morning in June when we discovered a mass of red poppies had sprouted up in the patio beds. I was up early munching my marmalade toast when he came in clutching a handful of the glorious, saucer-shaped orbs.

'Aren't they gorgeous?' he said gleefully, as the early morning sunlight beamed through the door like a celestial strobe. 'Your mother must have disturbed an old seed bank when she was weeding. I see the bees and hoverflies have already discovered them.'

After breakfast, I went outside to admire the wall of poppies. Sure enough, there were at least half a dozen honeybees buzzing around the scarlet blooms.

'They look drunk,' I said to my father, who had come to join me.

'They are,' he replied, swatting one of the dopier bees off my jumper.

I was distracted suddenly by a tiny flash of movement at the base of the bird table and, looking down, I saw Charlie, our resident mouse, dashing into a small hole in the terrace wall; he was carrying what looked suspiciously like part of a Cadbury's chocolate bar.

'Is that my chocolate?' I screamed at Dad. He was always feeding Charlie treats in the morning and it wasn't the first time he had left a sugary snack; yesterday I caught Charlie sneaking off with the tail end of a Battenberg cake.

'It might be,' he called guiltily from the flower bed, 'but I didn't think you wanted it. It's been sitting around for weeks.' Then, changing the subject, he said: 'Why don't we take Gazelle for a walk behind the house? We might find some more poppies in the field.'

'Can we take a peep at the haunted house on the way?' I said, cheering up. The house had been a constant source of fascination for my brother and me after rumours started circulating a few years back that a light had been seen in one of the upstairs windows accompanied by strange nocturnal noises. With my head fuelled with the adventures of Enid Blyton's *Famous Five*, I was convinced that an escaped convict was living in the attic.

We passed the front of the house on our way up the lane to the cornfield and noticed the broken wooden door had eerily blown open, allowing us to see over the threshold and into the dark, shadowy interior. To my amazement, I could see the hall and staircase had been engulfed in vegetation and that a tree or large shrub had penetrated the wooden floorboards and found light through an open window.

Seeing my surprise, Dad whispered in my ear, 'That's what happens when you abandon your house; it gets taken over by nature. I bet the whole place is crawling with plants and tiny creatures.'

'Could there be something else living there?' I said nervously. 'Perhaps there's a wild animal or a convict?'

'Well, maybe foxes and mice and some very large spiders, but as for convicts, I doubt it unless the farmer is storing one away,' Dad replied, with a smile.

'The same farmer who was peeping at Mum sunbathing topless on the patio last month?' I said glibly.

'That's the one. I have told your mother about Cyril but she still insists on stripping off. Doesn't want a bikini line when we go on holiday in August, apparently!'

I dragged my father away from the spooky house and we resumed our walk up the wooded footpath to the field.

Emerging from the shelter of the trees, we were hit by a sudden gush of hot air and had to shield our eyes from the bright sunlight. In front of us was a sea of butter-yellow wheat rimmed with a Union Jack strip of crimson poppies, electric-blue cornflowers and white campion.

'How amazing,' I said eventually, as we stood and stared. 'It's like the wheat has been transformed into a field of remembrance.'

On the way back, Daddy explained how the strip of wildflowers attracts butterflies and bees that in turn eat the aphids and other pests that would normally destroy the crops.

'Nature's clever that way. The pollinators are happy, the wildflowers are happy because they continue to get pollinated and the farmer is happy (or he should be). The only loser is the aphid but we don't care too much about him,' he added jocularly.

As we left the field, we saw a large tortoiseshell butterfly land on one of the red poppies – the first I had ever seen – and I rushed home, eager to include my new discoveries in my nature diary.

I'm back looking at the old family photo album when I stumble across a stunning photograph of my mother with Sam and Olivia in a field of crimson poppies.

The children are carrying plastic buckets and are in their pyjamas, which suggests it was past their bedtime and my mother was taking them on an evening adventure. She is beaming from ear to ear, her eyes dancing out from beneath a large, floral hat.

Sam and Olivia would have been thrilled to be doing something different. I can see them now, racing down to the gate, leaving a faint trail of golden sand spilled from their buckets on the grass, frolicking like fox cubs in the fading strobes of sunlight. They would have continued their chase through the cemetery like a couple of sparring spitfires while Mum and I tagged along behind, soaking up the countryside in all its glory.

I remember the shock of discovering the field of poppies, the sea of crimson, when we emerged from the shadows of the kissing gate onto the footpath. It was like a scene from an impressionist painting – acres and acres of red, stretching as far as the eye could see. Normally our fields would have been filled with yellow corn or rapeseed, or ploughed and brown, never scarlet, and whatever lay behind this vision of beauty, whether it was serendipity or intent, the local farmer had done us proud.

'Now that's what I call spectacular,' my mother said, snapping away with her instamatic camera. 'Tomorrow, I will bring my oils down here and paint this glorious scene.'

Staring at the photo again, I'm saddened that our countryside lacks the vibrancy it once had. Even without poppies, there are so few wildflowers left. Our hay meadows are gone and our lives are duller for it. I make up my mind, in this moment of reflection, that whatever I do or don't achieve in my revived wildlife garden, I will always leave a section, a small space for red poppies in memory of that special evening and my own childhood cornfield adventure.

NINE

WILD LAWNS
AND BIKINIS

Georgie is sniffing out mice and insects in the garden shed, and I'm rummaging around for a pair of gardening gloves. The air is still heavy from yesterday's storm but the sun is back out, at least for the time being.

I find some gloves and fill the mower with petrol. According to my wildlife garden book, the first step in creating a wildflower meadow is to clear the grass of any debris. This is known as scarifying. Because I've chosen to convert part of an existing lawn, I also need to excavate areas of bare earth where I can sow the wildflower seed directly into the soil. This should give the seed a greater chance of germinating, assuming the birds don't get there first.

I'm in no doubt that creating a meadow is going to take me several days and be pretty arduous, but at least I've started early enough in the season. I need to get the wildflower seed sown by the end of the autumn if I want my meadow to blossom next summer.

Even with the mower on the highest setting, I have to stop regularly to remove wet grass and moss from the blades, but I've brought my music with me and am spurred on by the upbeat country vocals of Josh Thompson.

An inquisitive robin follows behind me, scooping up the worms that have innocently ventured to the surface, and I'm being watched by a large red kite circling overhead. The hungry raptor hovers in the air like a glider, eying me suspiciously until a gang of angry rooks appear from nowhere, scaring it off with their cackling caws.

I often see a kite in our garden. Oxfordshire is full of them after a worried conservationist reintroduced them several years ago. Since then, their numbers have ballooned, and they are nearly as common in these parts as a gull or blackbird. If the kite can rebound this quickly, then it must be good news for the rest of nature and, in particular, for my meadow. Just by creating a small area of wildflowers, I could be increasing the life chances of 4,000 different species (up to forty species per square metre, according to my guide). I could be saving precious bumblebees, moths, butterflies, hover flies, shrews, voles, glow-worms, centipedes, grasshoppers, ants, hedgehogs and many more threatened species.

Who knows, I may even see a green woodpecker back in the garden, foraging for ants, a grass snake gliding through the undergrowth or a tortoiseshell butterfly sucking nectar from the wildflowers. If Ron's garden is anything to go by, I should, at the very least, have a beautiful, fertile field filled with colour and scent.

By tea-time, the rain has become quite persistent and I'm beginning to wilt. The damp has penetrated through to my skin, and every time the mower propels itself forward, my feet slip on the soggy soil, leaving skid marks on the newly cut grass. Time to retreat to the comfort of my sofa for a much-needed cup of tea and a slice of chocolate cake. I've taken a leaf out of my father's book and stocked up on sugary treats. No job is too arduous in the garden, he would say, if it ends in chocolate.

I call across the garden to Georgie who is busy scurrying around in the bushes for a pheasant. She looks up, her fur matted with beech leaves and grass. She gives herself a good shake and rushes up to greet me. Back in the kitchen, she gets a large chocolate dog treat and I cut myself a super-large slice of cake, and then we snuggle up together on the sofa and I dream of wheatfields and poppy meadows, while Georgie lies by my side licking the chocolate off my cheek.

I'm dressed early the next morning, eager to get outside and resume my meadow. I notice the grass is glistening with moisture after yesterday's rain and there's a light scattering of autumn leaves. A loud buzzing alerts me to a solitary bumblebee flying past the front door and making a beeline for Ron's nectar-rich garden.

'He won't be bee-passing us next year,' I joke to Georgie, who's rubbing up against my knee and wagging her long fan tail expectantly. We would normally be going on our walk about now but since I've started the meadow and the weather forecast is promising, I'm keen to continue scarifying while I can.

I'm dressed in a tatty old waxed jacket of Ed's which I found tucked away at the back of a cupboard, a billowing pair of waterproof trousers and oversized heavy brown boots (just like Ron's), and hoping my mother doesn't drop by for a cup of coffee.

Having been a fashion model in her early twenties, Mum's always been fastidious with her appearance and often critical of mine. She would always dress up rather than down to do the gardening when I was a child. I remember her wearing a glamorous Yves Saint Laurent bikini, pearl necklace and wide-brimmed hat to weed the flowerbed on her terrace, while her Twiggy-style mini skirt, complete with long false eye lashes and white knee-length boots was often her attire of choice to do the mowing. She refused to step outside the front door before styling her striking auburn locks into a fashionable neat bob and applying bright red lipstick. 'I would rather be seen naked than without my lippy, darling,' she often confided in me, puckering her striking crimson lips and blowing me a kiss. Even now, in her mid-eighties, she looks immaculate most of the time and insists on having her hair washed and blow-dried once a week at the local salon. I can imagine her response to my shocking outfit today:

'Well, if the wildlife scarpers, you'll know why. You might get away with that in the bushes darling, but nowhere else; you look like a tramp!'

I labour away for most of the morning, scraping at the stubborn grass and squidgy moss with my hoe and removing unwanted stones and sticks. It's hot work, and the soil is laden with large pieces of chalk, which makes the job harder still. The moss comes away easily with the rake but removing the tough clumps of grass is backbreaking and I'm forced to stop regularly for a stretch. Yesterday's demanding mow has clearly taken its toll on my weak muscles.

After a reviving cup of tea and an injection of sugar, I reluctantly head back to my raking; this time accompanied by the dulcet tones of Simon & Garfunkel's *Bridge over Troubled Water*. Very appropriate, I feel. I now know why Ron looks so hunched and weary most of the time in his garden.

As the music lulls me into a pleasant rhythm, I watch Ron through our dividing beech hedge labouring away in his own garden. He's holding a large pitchfork and staring at something in his vegetable patch and I can hear him mumbling disconcertingly to himself. I call across but he doesn't hear me. Clearly he's forgotten or not bothered again with his hearing aid.

We both carry on, absorbed in our separate projects until the light begins to fade and a grey mist descends on the trees. In a few weeks' time it will be too dark at this time to do any work in the garden.

What a difference a day makes. The rain is bucketing down and yesterday's positivity has all but abandoned me. I've chosen to put my feet up and spend the day reading on the sofa. Feeling equally forlorn, having been denied a walk for two days, Georgie reluctantly lies down on the chair next to me, resting her cold, wet nose on my knee. I've got the television on, and the news is depressing. A new state of nature report has found that over forty per cent of our wildlife in the UK is threatened with extinction (one in ten species has gone already) and our once nature-rich country is fast becoming one of the most wildlife-depleted places on the planet. The facts laid out starkly like that fill me with horror and I'm suddenly furious with our leaders for ignoring nature and with myself and others from my generation for not doing more, sooner and quicker, to change the way we live and protect our natural world.

'If our world is dying, we only have ourselves to blame,' I say angrily to Georgie, who has rolled over onto her back and fallen asleep. 'We're all bloody idiots!'

Later that evening, I'm researching online for UK-produced wildflower seed when I come across another shattering statistic that depresses me even more. According to recent studies, over ninety-seven per cent of all our wildflower meadows in the UK have disappeared since the 1930s thanks, largely, to intensive farming and human development. The sadness is that with each meadow lost, we also lose a vital ecosystem filled with irreplaceable wildlife, and the cycle of nature's decline intensifies. I remember my father's heartfelt plea in his letter, his fear that so-called 'progress' was destroying our natural world and I sense my resolve intensifying.

Meadows were magical places when I was growing up in the 1970s. I remember family walks in the water meadows that stretched for miles along the Medway. My brother and I loved to wade through the long grass with sticks, releasing clouds of insects and pollen while Gazelle hunted for mice and rabbits in the dense undergrowth. We often returned home covered in wildflower seeds but clutching posies of pretty flowers. In my teens, I remember sneaking into the meadow across the road from our house with my school friends, laden with bottles of beer and wine from my father's booze cupboard. Unbeknown to him, we would carouse and canoodle in the long grass to the sound of the bees and crickets and skylarks singing overhead. The only interruption was the occasional roar of a car on the steep hill behind us or the peel of bells from the Norman church across the valley.

Wildflower meadows were a bedrock of the English countryside back then, a feature of our childhoods that we took for granted. I find it inconceivable that in just a few years, they may all have disappeared. The realisation fills me with horror, but for the first time in months I can see a clear path ahead. I have a fresh incentive to wild my garden and there will be no turning back.

I wake to a beautiful orange sunrise and a garden dappled with sunlight. The lawn is still moist from the early morning dew and the bare patches in my burgeoning meadow are almost translucent in the sun. I yank on a tatty pair of leggings and race downstairs to grab some toast and a quick cup of coffee. Georgie is itching for some exercise, so I grab her lead as soon as I've finished breakfast and head straight out. We take the footpath through the cemetery down into the field which is now a brown expanse of ploughed furrows. At the bottom of the valley, we pass through the turnstile that leads to a pretty beech and pine wood, which is popular with walkers. It's quiet today, and I take a moment to breathe in the fresh, sappy scents before ascending the grassy slope by the side of the wood to join the footpath above. Despite being mid-October, the meadow still has wildflowers in bloom and the air is teeming with flying ants, moths and other insects.

I've brought my *Observer's Book of Wild Flowers* to help me identify some of the meadow species. I'm hoping it will give me an idea of what grows well on chalk uplands and what wildflowers to buy for my own meadow. Up ahead, I see a narrow deer track snaking through the meadow. I follow it, descending towards the arable field below, marking off in my little book the species I see along the way. I'm amazed how many flowers are still in bloom and when I get up close and divide the grass, I find blue sheep's bit, feathery yarrow, white and red clover, pink dropwort, cow parsley, wild marjoram, bird's-foot trefoil and thistle. Some have faded blooms, but the long, dry summer has clearly helped others extend their flowering period. Among the flowers are a few hungry bees enjoying the late nectar including a buff-tailed, white-tailed and several honey varieties.

Ascending back up the slope, I notice patches of teasel growing in the long grass, their spiky flowerheads swaying in the breeze like oversized bottle brushes. I can't identify all the flowers, some are simply too withered, but I have enough ideas now for my own meadow.

Ron is at the end of the drive when I get home, sweeping up the first of the autumn leaves. He peers out from under his floppy hat as I pass and pats Georgie on the nose. 'All right there, love? How's the wildlife meadow coming on?' He's surrounded by round neat piles of leaves that dot the drive like colourful stepping stones.

'Good thanks, Ron. Tough on the old back but then I'm not the fittest.' I bring him up to date with my progress at the bottom of the garden. 'I'm almost finished with the preparation, but there's too much grass and I'm a bit worried my wildflower seed will get suffocated.'

'You need yellow rattle, dear. It acts like a parasite on the grass, smothering the roots and halting its spread. I use it all the time on my grass, and it's a pretty wildflower too with lots of pollen and nectar for the insects. Sow it now, and it will germinate nicely by spring.'

I'd not heard of yellow rattle, but Ron's suggestion sounds sensible and so I rush back home to research how I can purchase some quickly. Seeing the autumn leaves has reminded me that time is running out if I want to get my wildlife garden completed before the onset of winter. I've still got a pond, plants, bulbs, compost heaps and insect houses to make in less than two months. I heat up some soup and a roll and sit down to ponder my next move. As has been the case every day recently, I think first of what my father would do and then refer to my list of tasks on the fridge.

The day after my yellow rattle seed arrives, Ron knocks on the door and we walk down to the meadow together with Georgie. He's prepared a large wheelbarrow full of soil and sand and I've got a bag of seed under my arm. I'm intrigued about the sand, and he explains it will help reduce the nutrients in the soil, which is essential for wildflowers.

I watch closely as he mixes everything together, breaking up the clumps of soil with his knobbly fingers as if he's a chef again making a mountain of crumble. I feel incredibly fortunate to have his help. Given the scale of all the tasks I have set myself, I'm not sure I could tackle them alone and, in a strange way, I feel I am helping him too. It's a project for him as much as for me and company for us both.

Together we sprinkle the seed lightly over the bare soil, and when he starts pressing it down with his boot, I see my father doing the same with his flower seeds over forty years ago. He would be eighty in January, but it seems only yesterday that he was showing me how to grow plants from seed by pressing them gently into compost with the tip of a finger. I was so proud of my tray of seeds that I would check on their progress every day until they were big enough to be planted out. My old nature diary comes to mind, and I wonder if my letter has arrived at the old family home and if they have checked the attic.

I remember the exact moment I discovered how worried my father was about nature. He liked to chart moth and butterfly populations in the garden and would share his analysis with me, but this particular year I saw him ripping up his recordings and swearing loudly as he threw them in the bin. He called me into his study eventually and explained with deep sadness in his eyes that lepidoptera numbers were down again, and he blamed the harmful pesticides farmers were putting on their crops. 'It's madness!' he exclaimed, slamming his hand down on his desk. 'They're ruining our countryside with these chemicals and nothing is being done about it.'

He had tears in his eyes then and I feel my own sadness returning. I pick up a handful of Ron's seeds and chuck it aggressively across the grass out of frustration more than anything else, narrowly missing Ron's head.

'Watch it, dear!' he shouts, 'you're not swatting flies.'

Georgie suddenly appears from nowhere and starts charging after a large bird she has flushed out of the beech hedge; it's a terrified pheasant that must have sneaked into the bottom of our garden unnoticed. I rush forwards just in time to see her grabbing the squawking fowl by its long tail. 'Off that!' I scream, but she's in full hunting mode and has her jaws firmly clamped around the pheasant's juicy rump. I flap my hands and, just as a massacre looks inevitable, the bird breaks free and, like a rocket released from its pad, soars heavenwards through a web of overhanging branches. As it disappears into the ether, a confused and distraught Georgie turns to face us, her mouth a matted knot of long elegant tail feathers.

'Well, you'll have to sort that bloody dog out, dear, if you want a wildlife garden,' Ron says, leaning on his garden fork and smiling broadly.

I don't disagree.

After the last few drops of seed have gone into the soil, Ron stamps the earth flat with the back of his boot, making sure that each patch is firmly bedded down. 'Your biggest problem will be keeping the birds off the seeds,' he says, as I join in the stamping. 'Just keep adding more seed each year and don't expect miracles. Nature wins sometimes, you just need to be patient.'

Sitting out on my terrace later, I close my eyes and listen to the sea-surge of wind in the tall trees. I can smell the woody aroma of Ron's bonfire. I'm reminded again of my childhood and my father's bonfires and, for a few blissful moments, I'm completely lost in revery.

TEN

STORM CLOUDS

The wind and heavy rain have stopped and I go outside to rake some leaves for Dad's bonfire. I breathe in the delicious aroma of smouldering leaves and damp wood and it reminds me of the recent Brownie camp I went on when we roasted sausages, chestnuts and apples over a large fire built from gathered fir cones, fallen sticks and dry leaves. By the oak tree, I notice there are hundreds of acorns. They make a scrunching sound, like shells on a beach, as I stomp over them in my wellingtons. I call Dad over, and he is as surprised as me. 'That's a lot of acorns. It must be a mast year.'

'What's that?' I ask.

'It's when the oak tree produces a bumper crop of fruit. It only happens after a dry spring and it's to ensure the oak survives as a species. In any normal year, mice, squirrels, jays and rooks will whip the acorns before they can grow into new trees but in a mast year, there are so many acorns that at least one or two usually survive. It's one of nature's little miracles.'

I mull over this strange phenomenon as I continue to collect up the leaves. A small robin comes to join me and I watch as he rummages around under the leaves for worms.

Dad and I love the autumn. I love the fact the trees go all colours of the rainbow, and he loves to have a bonfire. If he's not having a bonfire, he's chopping wood for the winter or piling up his compost with leaves and dead headings for the insects and hedgehogs to hibernate in. This means more worms which is good news for our robin.

'Why don't we go to Bluebell Wood after lunch?' he suggests. 'The trees will be at their best, and Gazelle needs a walk.'

'Can we play Poohsticks in the stream?'

'Of course, if you help me finish up here first.'

After one of Mum's delicious roast dinners – chicken and sizzling roast potatoes followed by blackberry and apple crumble – we set off down the hill in Dad's 1950s Morris Minor. Gazelle and I are squeezed against each other on the back seat. She leans across me affectionately as the Morris labours up the first hill and puffs warm smelly breath over my face, forcing me to open a window. As I close my eyes and suck in the fresh air, she squeezes her face against mine and snorts loudly, her ears flapping, like sails in the wind.

The wood is littered with debris from the strong Atlantic storm that passed through two nights ago and the waterlogged fields glisten in the afternoon sunlight. But the trees are still a kaleidoscope of yellow, coppery-orange, maroon and red. We take the same shadowy footpath we always take through the labyrinth of oak, lime and fir, and Dad points out the trees that have fallen victim to the storm. There is one gargantuan oak that has split, spectacularly, in two and fallen like a fairy tale giant across the stream.

In the spring, this ancient forest is a carpet of azure bluebells but today, after one of the worst autumn storms ever recorded, it's like a battlefield of fallen soldiers. The sun is only just peeping through the thick canopy of leaves and branches, and the cold air smells damp and peaty.

'Of course, all these fallen trees and big branches will eventually decay and make wonderful homes for mice, hedgehogs, woodpeckers, bats and kestrels,' he says, trying to sound cheerful, but I can tell he is shocked. The storm has wreaked devastation on our wood on a biblical scale.

We continue along the footpath until we reach the bubbling brook and the small wooden bridge where we like to play our game. Poohsticks was invented by Winnie the Pooh and involves each person dropping a small twig or stick over a bridge and then racing to other side to see which emerges first.

Today, the torrent is higher than usual and it's almost impossible to reach the opposite side of the bridge before both our sticks disappear out of sight, shooting off downstream like a couple of miniature kayaks in a rapid. But it's still fun. Dad and I play at least a dozen times before Gazelle decides she's had enough and plunges into the cold water to steal the sticks.

At the end of the walk, Dad waits while I fill my pockets with shiny bright conkers from a massive horse chestnut tree at the edge of the wood. Fresh from their cosy kernels that are littering the ground, they look like precious jewels and when we get home, I line them up on the windowsill in my bedroom like trophies.

It's dawn, and the rain is relentless, drenching the barren garden and clouding the air in a bonfire mist. The storm has denuded the trees of their autumn colour and the terrace outside the back door has disappeared under a sea-surge of water.

I didn't sleep well. I've been having some disturbing dreams recently and last night I dreamt I was being sucked into a deep, muddy sink hole with nobody around to save me. Just when I thought I was about to disappear into the mire, I saw my father's face and felt his strong arm reaching down to pull me free. I must have cried out in my sleep because the next thing I knew, Ed was holding me tightly in his arms, soothing my heated brow with soft finger brush strokes.

I still worry that I've left my wilding project too late. The scale of biodiversity loss seems to worsen by the day. It's now feared that over half our bumblebee and two-thirds of our moth and butterfly species have declined (some by more than fifty per cent) since my childhood in the 1970s. Our native birds too are in serious trouble and some of my father's favourite species when I was a young girl – the skylark, turtle dove and the nightingale – are almost extinct in Britain today. The gloom eats away at me over breakfast, and still lingers as I set out for my early morning walk with Georgie.

By the time I reach the cemetery stile, my cheeks are frozen and rigid from the biting wind, my eyes are streaming from the driving rain and my glasses have all misted up. I stop to wipe my lenses and Georgie sidles up to me, rubbing her long nose against the back of my knee as if she senses my sombre mood. I haven't stroked her for a while so I give her a reassuring rub on the back of her neck. She immediately responds by licking my face and fanning me with her tail. We continue the walk together, slip-sliding our way along the muddy footpath as it dips down towards the village. My view across the fields is entirely obscured by a curtain of thick rain being pulled across the hillside by the wind and the only sound in the distance is the gentle whoosh of cars on the road to the M4.

The sudden gush of a fast train to London jolts me alert, reminding me that the world is waking up to another busy workday and, however much I fret about the natural world declining, the unstoppable progress of our lives continues, unchallenged and relentless. We cross an empty playing field where local football teams battle it out in finer weather and then turn left when we reach the road. A few hardy joggers and cyclists scoot past and up the steep hill to the farm, their Lycra outfits splattered with mud.

As we climb the hill, I have to manoeuvre through a torrent and avoid the large potholes that have completely disappeared in the muddy water and, by the time we reach the stile by the field which leads back home, I'm soaked to the skin and Georgie's fur has stuck to her back like a black silky coat. Her strained expression tells me she's not enjoying the walk at all and would much prefer to be back home snug on the sofa.

I stop at the stile and look up. The rain has begun to subside a little and I glimpse a hopeful, blue gap forming between the clouds. In another minute, the sun will be out.

The hill is steep and I can feel the sweat building up under my warm jumper. I remove my jacket, fling it over my shoulder and continue purposefully to the top, aware of my heart pounding more and more as I increase my strides near the top. Georgie is panting too, trying to keep pace and her whole body is shrouded in a steamy cloud rising off her damp fur. The more I sweat, the more the tension in me seems to dissipate and, little by little, I feel my mind clearing like the afternoon rain.

At the turnstile, I stop and take a deep breath before turning to admire the view. From my lofty position, I can see right down the Thames Valley, from Pangbourne in the south to Didcot in the north. It amazes me to think that this wooded gorge is as ancient as the last mammoths that roamed this land. It was carved out by a giant glacier at the end of the last ice age when the ice melted and slipped away through the chalk. The Thames was formed then along with the woods and water meadows that still exist on both sides of the river. I notice, with some relief, that the sun has lit up Chalk Hill in the distance, the only field in a wall of ancient woodland that marks the start of the North Wessex Downs.

On my left is Hartslock Nature Reserve, set back on a chalky hillside above the valley. Last summer, Ed and I walked across it and saw some rare monkey and lady orchids that the local wildlife trust is eagerly trying to conserve. We also saw some other rare, wonderfully-named specimens that mark this area of Oxfordshire: Pasqueflower, bastard toadflax and snake's head fritillary.

The clouds have cleared and, as I look up to admire the indigo blue dome above me, I'm reminded of how big the cosmos is with its millions of galaxies and how old our planet is compared to my tiny, fleeting existence on earth.

It seems to me that, since inception 4.5 billion years ago, Earth has constantly been regenerating; it has faced seismic threats from ice ages, floods, meteorites and other extreme events, yet nature has always managed to bounce back, somehow. Like a phoenix springing from the ashes, life has returned whatever slings and arrows the cosmos has thrown at it. The thought gives me hope.

Leaving my ancient landscape behind, I feel calmer. The fresh air and quiet meditation have brought me to my senses, and my childhood faith in nature has been temporarily restored. I resume my walk along the crest of the hill, enjoying the warm sun; the breeze has dropped, and I tune in to the chorus of happy birdsong.

Later that afternoon, I dig out some of my favourite novels about nature and start by rereading one of Thomas Hardy's masterpieces – *The Return of the Native*. Thomas Hardy was a fervent naturalist writing about agrarian England just after the Industrial Revolution and he often depicted, with remarkable luminosity, our bucolic forebears' connection with nature and their respect for their past:

To recline on a stump of thorn in the central valley of Egdon, between afternoon and night, as now, where the eye could reach nothing of the world outside the summits and shoulders of heathland which filled the whole circumference of its glance, and to know that everything around and underneath had been from pre-historic times as unaltered as the stars overhead… The great inviolate place had an ancient permanence which the sea cannot claim.

ELEVEN

BUG LOVE

I couldn't wait to create my very own garden. Dad had helped me clear a patch of the front flowerbed and given me six small pots of flowers grown from seed and a packet of wildflower seed. It was hot work as the ground was rock hard after weeks of dry weather.

'I think we're heading for another drought,' my father said ruefully, as he levered out the tough weeds with his garden fork. 'And you know what that means? More hosepipe bans.'

'Oh no,' I whispered under my breath. That meant more of my father's ridiculous attempts to conserve water. Last summer, during the worst drought in decades, Dad devised a highly complicated and ultimately flawed scheme to conserve the bath water so he could reuse it to water his vegetables. It involved diverting the water from the bath using a hose from the downpipe into a large wheelbarrow strategically placed on the grass below. The problem was it relied on me pulling the bath plug and releasing the water at

precisely the right moment. If I got it wrong, and I did most of the time, my father got drenched with dirty, soapy water and would scream up at me as I hid in the bathroom. This scheme lasted most of the summer of 1976 until my father's broad beans and lettuces eventually withered in the blistering heat, despite our best efforts.

Having experienced first-hand the deprivation of the Second World War, Dad found waste of any kind abhorrent, and would go beyond the bounds of reason to conserve everything.

'You never know when it might come in useful,' was his famous mantra. Baths were a form of torture – usually tepid with only enough water to cover our legs, and always shared. He became apoplectic if the water was let out before at least three family members had shared it, and until we rebelled as teenagers, he insisted we only had one bath a week. A large stone paddling pool doubled up as an alternative bath for a few weeks in the summer until it became dangerously-fetid and green with algae.

I noticed a thin layer of sweat had formed on Dad's brow, and his shirt was sticking to his shoulders. He had just a few stones left to remove from my garden and I was lining them up around the bare patch, like a fence. The earth felt good between my fingers; it smelt fresh and spicy and reminded me of building sandcastles on the beach.

A big hairy spider suddenly appeared from under a stone and ran across my leg. 'Get it off,' I shrieked, swiping at my legs and jumping up and down. Dad leant down and scooped the spider up in his hands before I had a chance to stamp it with my feet.

I hated spiders at that age, but not quite as much as I hated the big red biting ants that seemed to emerge from every nook and cranny in our garden. When we were very small, Simon and I would fill large plastic bottles with boiling water and look for ant nests to destroy. We would pour the burning liquid over the poor creatures and watch while they writhed and squirmed in agony. My father was furious when he found out.

'Have you any idea how cruel that is!' he screamed at us. 'Poor ants, imagine how you would feel having boiling water poured over you. Ants have feelings too, you know.'

We didn't care at that age – we were just kids having fun – and surreptitiously kept our little game going until the novelty eventually wore off.

After the soil was prepared, I dug six flowerpot-sized holes and planted my seedlings side by side, bedding them down firmly. I then sprinkled the wildflower seed liberally over the bare patches before filling my can with water and giving the new garden a good soaking. I couldn't wait to see my flowers magically bloom.

As I stood up and admired my creation, a small tortoiseshell butterfly fluttered down and settled onto a blue cornflower, its spotted wing tips iridescent in the sunlight. I watched, mesmerised as it sank its long, dark proboscis into the flower's centre and stayed firmly pinned to the flowerhead. I hoped my little garden would attract many more butterflies and moths in the months to come.

In bed that night, Dad read me a passage from Frances Hodgson Burnett's *The Secret Garden* as I lay back and imagined fairies discovering my own secret flower garden.

Magic is always pushing and drawing and making things out of nothing. Everything is made out of magic, leaves and trees, flowers and birds, badgers and foxes and squirrels and people. So it must be all around us. In this garden – in all places.

It's the first official day of autumn – 21 October – and a full month since I started my wilding project.

The garden is strewn with leaves and branches after another violent storm in the night and the grass has become a mushy field of mud. In the past I would have chucked all the fallen debris on a bonfire, or disposed of it in a bin, but today I'm collecting up the sticks and branches to use in my new "insect hotel". The hotel is an idea from my wildlife gardening book, inspired by concerns over the widespread decline of insects, particularly bees.

As wildlife projects go, the insect hotel looks relatively straightforward and a good option for a rainy day.

I find a semi-shady spot in a tucked away part of the garden and start with the main structure; this consists of three wooden pallets (left over from a delivery of fertiliser last year) which I stack one on top of the other with a thin piece of timber squeezed between each pallet to make a floor. I create the hotel roof by layering old tiles over a sheet of waterproof lining. Finally, I fill all the gaps with tatty bits of old material, plastic bottles, halved and filled with corrugated cardboard, moss, sticks, bamboo, petals, desiccated flowerheads and leaves. My father would be proud to see me making use of nature's off-cuts and bits and bobs from the house that would otherwise have ended up in the dustbin and, with luck, my hotel will be a heaving mass of insect activity in a few months. It might even attract mason and leafcutter bees, lacewings and butterflies and other over-wintering species.

The finished hotel reminds me of the houses my father built for hedgehogs in our garden in Kent and which I filled with straw and newspaper and saucers of food and water.

Fifty years ago, the countryside was teeming with invertebrates and it was not uncommon for our car windscreen to be splattered with carcasses at the end of even the shortest of journeys. It saddens me to think that many of the insect species I grew up with are now quite scarce: earwigs, grasshoppers, crickets, stag beetles, centipedes and millipedes as well as an alarming number of pollinating insects. As my father once told me, all these creatures have their role to play in the rich tapestry of life and if my garden is to become rich again in biodiversity, I need to make an extra special effort to encourage them.

Another of my father's winter jobs was to create natural log piles around the garden to ensure the wildlife had adequate protection and food. Rotting wood is vital for many species including frogs, toads, hedgehogs, lizards and even snakes. As they decay, the logs attract moss and fungi which is a vital food source for many invertebrates as well as essential nesting material for garden birds. There's ample space for log piles along our boundary fence, but despite searching behind every bush and shed, I only uncover a few loose logs and most of these are decaying already. I leave them where they are, reluctant to disrupt the limited insect life I already have and head indoors for some lunch.

Ron comes round later with some logs of his own. He shows me how to stack them in a pyramid shape which creates large gaps that the larger creatures can crawl into. It's hard work lugging the logs from his garage to the end of my garden and I can see he's staggering a bit and looking tired. Occasionally, he stops to catch his breath and mop the sweat off his brow. The last time we spoke, he said he'd been suffering from neuralgia and I'm worried that the pain in his face might be worsening each time he helps me with some arduous job.

'Are you feeling well, Ron?' I say tentatively as he places a particularly large log on the ground in front of me. 'You look tired today. Please don't hang round if you want to get some rest. I can manage, I really can, and Ed will be home soon.'

'It's okay, dear, it's just the pain in my head; it gets to me sometimes,' he replies, smiling and tipping his hat in his usual way.

TWELVE

RUN, RABBIT, RUN!

My father was usually delighted when wildlife visited our garden. If he saw a roe deer, a fox, a badger, stoat or shrew, he would grab his field glasses and track the creature around the garden as if he were on safari, but when it came to rabbits, my father turned from enthusiastic naturalist into crazed murderer. His nickname was "Mr McGregor" for good reason. Thankfully for the white-tailed bunnies spotted in our garden, their warren was next door in our neighbour's field and if they did manage to sneak through our fence in pursuit of my father's carrots and tasty flowers, they were never really in any danger. Dad's military training hadn't paid off when it came to firearms and despite numerous attempts to shoot the rabbits with his vintage air rifle, they still managed to reign supreme, wreaking havoc in the garden.

Dad blamed the warped sights on his gun for all his failed attempts to kill the rabbits, but this was just an excuse. We knew my father well enough not to argue on such a sensitive subject and would simply keep our distance whenever we saw him rolling up his sleeves to take a pot shot.

I was sitting happily on the grass making daisy chains one summer's afternoon when four adorable bobtails appeared at the bottom of the garden under the oak tree. They started nibbling the long grass and hopping about merrily just like Flopsy, Mopsy, Cotton-tail and Peter in Beatrix Potter's tale of Peter Rabbit.

'Could you lend me a hand with this netting?' my father called to me from his vegetable patch. 'I want to keep the rabbits off my carrots.' I then heard him scream: 'Good God, cheeky bastards! How the bloody hell did they get in?'

Abandoning his work, Dad raced back to the house, visibly shaking with fury, to fetch his air rifle. I didn't dare shoo the rabbits away; the last time I tried that, he had been so angry, he threatened to lock me in my bedroom.

The wait was interminable but eventually his shiny egg head appeared at the bedroom window and the long metal barrel of his gun poked out, pointing resolutely in the direction of the oak tree. There was a loud pop followed by an ominous whizzing sound as a pellet soared through the air before hitting its unintended target. I looked up to see a piece of the oak tree bark ricocheting off into our neighbour's garden and then a loud "Shit!" resounding from the bedroom window, before the frame banged shut, and there was silence. The rabbits, by now, had skedaddled off back to their field.

Across the garden, on the other side of the fence, I could see our neighbour, Mr Blakemore, staring ferociously at me. His eyes were out like organ stops and he was waving his arms around like an octopus. For a ghastly moment I thought he had been shot.

'Tell your father from me that if I catch him firing his wretched air rifle in this direction again, I'll call the police! He could have killed me!'

I ran inside to warn my father but found him back in his study, oiling his gun. As I breathlessly repeated what the neighbour had said, he glared at me over the dark rim of his spectacles, his cheeks scarlet, and murmured: 'You tell Blakemore from me that if he doesn't control those bloody rabbits, I will stick my gun over his fence and shoot them, one by one!'

Decency and patience evaded my father when it came to rabbits, but when it came to cultivating a wildlife garden and, in particular, growing plants, he had the patience of Job. His garden was his sanctuary and his greenhouse the centre of that haven. After a long day working in London, he would retreat into the glass house for an hour, at least, to unwind and find peace. Only when he had heard the birds sing, watered his plants and weeded a border or sown some seeds would he come in for his evening meal. I loved it when he asked me to help him. It didn't matter if I was in my dressing gown and slippers, I still got to plant seeds or water pots and he always took the time to explain the plants to me and the best conditions for them. Absorbed in nature and each other, nothing else mattered.

Dad had a particular passion for roses, particularly the old English shrub variety, and grew them everywhere, up the front of the house, the garage and the sheds and even around the massive trunk of the oak. He also loved scented flowers and festooned the terrace with highly perfumed honeysuckles and philadelphus that were always a mass of bees and butterflies.

Tucked away in the orchard was a Victorian brick well which was still in working order when we first moved into the family home back in 1967. Simon and I would stand on tiptoes and scream into the deep chamber, listening for the sonorous echo of our voices. After the novelty of the well wore off, my father boarded up the hole and filled the top with pink and white primroses, pansies and wild strawberries. It became a picture-postcard focal point in the back garden and each year he would add more flowers to the display and we watched as the butterflies and bees descended on the rich nectar and pollen.

My father was full of creative ideas in the garden, but outside the confines of his sanctuary he had no real artistic ability and his lack of sartorial style, particularly when it came to colour sense, was legendary. My poor, fashionable mother was often left speechless by his outfits.

They were going out to a summer party one evening when he came downstairs dressed in maroon corduroy trousers, a light blue shirt and what looked suspiciously like orange loafers.

My mother's jaw hit the floor. 'You're not seriously thinking of wearing that combination to the Binders' are you, Timmy? They will never invite us back!'

Undeterred, he did what he always did when my mother got on her high horse, blew a large raspberry. 'I certainly am, and if you don't want to join me you can stay and eat fishfingers with the children.'

He loved winding my mother up and he was as stubborn as an old mule if challenged. My mother tried her best to influence him but, in the end, she gave up. 'Your father always knows best,' she would say with exasperation.

Each week before the bins were collected, Dad would rifle through the rubbish, retrieving bits and bobs that my mother had thrown away – perfume bottles, vanity cases, broken cups, jam jars or boxes – and then store them in his shed in case they came in handy at a later date.

'The bees will love these,' he said one day, sprinkling echinacea and cosmos seeds into an old hiking boot he had filled with soil and then hung from a tree. Another time, he converted a broken toolbox into a hedgehog shelter and left it under some bushes by the garage, although I never saw an actual hedgehog visit.

One of the best things he restored was an old carriage wheel which had been left in the garden by the previous owner. After it was beautified, Dad propped it up against the front of the house and grew a pretty "Rambling Rector" rose through its spokes. 'The Rector is climbing the wall again,' he would say, jocularly, every time the rose grew a little further up the whitewashed frontage. Another of his quirkier ideas was to adapt the remains of a coach chassis into a plant support. He called it his "classical sculpture", plonked it right in the centre of the terrace (to my mother's horror) and grew a scented hyacinth up through the middle. Old, cracked terracotta pots were reclaimed and reused for delphiniums, lupins and white phlox and he even converted a set of horse reins from the former stables into an unwieldly cotoneaster wall support. I remember how he beamed with delight when he saw a redwing using it to get a foothold on the plant.

THIRTEEN

BLOOMING
MARVELLOUS

After fetching a pair of strong wire clippers and donning my father's old leather knee protectors, I trudge down to the southern end of the garden, chatting to Ron. He's feeling much better after going to the pharmacy and getting some medication for his headaches. We're accompanied by an unexpectedly noisy dawn chorus.

'We all need to be able to roam freely,' Ron says whimsically as we reach the gate by the oak. 'It's no different for animals and birds. The bats you see in my garden, they need hedges for shelter, while hedgehogs, voles and shrews prefer long grass.'

He explains that a hedgehog will roam up to two kilometres every night in search of food, and without gaps in fences and long stretches of grass to keep them safe they become disorientated or, worse still, die, probably on a road.

'Hedgehog numbers have fallen drastically, dear, in recent years. There used to be nearly two million of the little blighters once upon a time but now, well, we're looking at probably just 500,000 remaining. It's sad really.'

I nod, guiltily, and hand him my clippers. He kneels down and scrapes away the autumn detritus from the base of our fence before cutting a large square hole in the wire. It's not soft chicken wire but strong animal-proof aluminium which Ed and I erected when we moved, eager to keep our pets and children safely ensconced in the garden. It never crossed our minds that we might be preventing hedgehogs, foxes, badgers, stoats and shrews from reaching their natural habitats or reducing their chances of finding a mate. By the time Ron and I have finished making the holes, my former impenetrable enclosure looks as if it's been bomb-blasted.

After lunch, Ron returns with a wheelbarrow filled with willow stems. He wants to demonstrate how to make a "dead" fence which he says will provide shelter for the wildlife as they roam through the garden.

'They're popular nesting sites for birds,' he explains as he weaves together two long willow stems, in the same way he might plait hair, until they form a long, low trellis-like structure. I'm impressed with his craftmanship.

'Where did you learn that, Ron?' I ask, genuinely interested.

'It's what we learnt growing up in Wales, dear. Our ancestors would have been masters at making dead hedges from willow in the days when it was still popular to coppice wood to make firewood and charcoal. They knew what they were doing in those days,' he adds nostalgically.

I'm so absorbed in watching Ron that I've barely noticed the dark shadows appearing in the garden. Georgie has already returned to the house, desperate for her supper. After the last stem has been wound into the fence, Ron tips his hat and returns to his garden while I pack away the tools in my shed. It feels good to know my garden is porous again and, later as I'm snuggled next to Georgie on the sofa reading my wildlife books, I envisage a queue of happy hedgehogs and badgers, rabbits and foxes lining up to go through the fence.

The next day, I complete the superhighway corridors by putting out saucers of food and water by the side of the holes for the travelling animals – a *bona fide* wildlife service station.

I've got my father's field glasses pinned on the silver birch in our back garden and I'm trying to identify the tiny birds jostling for space on the lower branches. On one sprawling mossy limb, I see several of the same species, their wings iridescent in the bright morning sunlight. They look like blue tits at first glance, but on closer inspection I see they have jet black heads and their tummies are mottled-white. Referring to my grandmother's glossy bird guide, I discover that they are probably willow tits – six in total – and I spend a restful afternoon watching them feeding and playing kiss chase in the back garden. Later that same day, I glimpse my first treecreeper spiralling up the silver birch, pecking, ferociously, at the ivy-clad trunk for grubs as the sun catches its silvery-grey back. I feel like a child again and rush to record the sighting in a new nature diary. My old childhood journal is still unfound but I remain hopeful it will reappear one day. I would never have dreamt, a few weeks ago, that I would be doing this, having moments of pure joy again absorbed in nature and writing, so soon after starting the wildlife project. My new-found enthusiasm forces me up earlier and earlier in the morning, sometimes before dawn, so eager am I to explore, listen and assess the progress of my fledgling garden.

'Your flowerbeds are the backbone of your garden,' Ron says philosophically as we chat casually over the gate one afternoon in early November. The garden is caked in a thick, grey fog and there's a xylophone at play under the trees as heavy dew drops ping onto the hard, leaf-strewn surface below. I've left the bulk of the autumn leaves to pile up for the wildlife as Ron suggested I should do.

'The plants you choose will make or break the garden and determine what birds and insects you attract. It may also make the difference between getting a hedgehog or not – any small mammal for that matter.'

I've got Ron's flower list with me and we're discussing what to buy. I don't want to leave the planting too late; the November forecast is not promising and my days gallivanting in the garden, whatever the weather, are waning fast with each passing shower.

Ron recommends, very sensibly, that I list the flowers according to when they bloom during the year; that way I will get my much hoped for all-year-round colour. We've sorted autumn between us. I've simply chosen many of the species still in bloom in his garden and we're currently thinking about winter.

'You want lots of bulbs to help your garden through the cold months and shrubs or roses with late-summer hips, berries and seeds. These will attract mammals, like badgers, voles and foxes, as well as birds and insects. It's all about getting the right mix, dear. Bushy shrubs and roses are also good for protecting vulnerable wildlife from predators, and don't forget some scented shrubs like honeysuckle and jasmine; they will draw the moths.'

I had forgotten about the moths. I scribble down Ron's suggestions and then go inside for a refreshing cup of coffee and a much-needed biscuit. I also need time to think. My list is getting long and I haven't even included the spring and summer plants. The last thing I want to do is spend a fortune on new flowers then find they fail because I don't have the time to look after them.

My flower books aren't helping either. There's so much choice that I'm going boss-eyed just looking at the pictures. I'm contemplating shelving the books altogether when I make a wonderful discovery. Tucked away in the bottom of my father's trunk is the *Oxford Book of Garden Flowers*.

I lift it out now and opening the cover, discover my father's scrawl on the inside front page and the words – *Dearest Annabel – for getting top marks in your school report. Enjoy! love Dad.* It's dated 1975, the year I turned ten which would have been at the height of our green odyssey together.

Flicking through the chapters, I see to my delight that the author has conveniently grouped the flower types according to the season they bloom. At last, a clear and straightforward guide to achieving diversity as well as all-year colour. I happily retire to my desk in the study and start making notes.

Picking out the best flowers for wildlife, however, is not so easy. I need to refer to my contemporary guidebooks and the internet for that. Gardening for wildlife was clearly not a priority for most British gardeners in the 1970s. My father was the exception, of course, but I can see from the Oxford flower book that it was more about aesthetics in those days.

The internet, particularly the website for my local Wildlife Trust, BBOWT and the Royal Horticultural Society's web pages are full of fascinating facts and figures. I learn, for example, that bees prefer blue, purple or mauve plants, while birds and butterflies are drawn to red, orange and yellow. Moths, on the other hand, (of which there are over 2,500 different species in the UK) are attracted to white and scented blooms like magnolia "grandiflora" and jasmine. The rich perfume coaxes them through the darkness to the rich nectar-filled stamens at the centre of the flowers.

But, like everything else I am learning about wildlife gardening, there is no hard-and-fast rule when it comes to choosing suitable flora for the garden, particularly when it comes to choosing native over non-native plants, or to put it another way – plants that are indigenous to the UK and those that have been imported from abroad.

Few experts would disagree that indigenous plants adapt better to changes in the environment, are less prone to disease and provide better habitats and food for our wildlife, but recent research by Rosi Rollings and Dave Goulson *(Journal of Insect Conservation)* also shows there is little difference in the diversity of flower-visiting insects to native cultivars than to non-native. Interestingly, the most-visited plants in the scientific study were calamintha nepeta (catmint), helenium autumnale (common sneezeweed), geranium "Rozanne" (cranesbill), borago officinalis (borage) and origanum vulgare (wild marjoram) and, rather surprisingly, insects from the same class did not always visit the same plant. In fact, on many occasions, similar plant cultivars attracted different pollinators. Seventy-two per cent of visiting insects, for instance, to the aster novi-belgii (Michaelmas daisy) were honeybees and bumblebees while anthemis tinctoria (marguerite), which also has daisy-shaped flowers, did not attract a single bumble or honeybee but was popular with solitary bees and hoverflies.

Diversity seems to be the key. After much pondering, I finally put together my shopping list of plants and stick the list on the fridge next to my garden objectives. I then grab my bag and head straight out to the nursery. 'Carpe diem,' my father would say. 'What are you waiting for? The early bird always catches the worm.'

Returning home, I put the Oxford flower book on the shelf with my other newly discovered childhood tomes, and then go back outside to start planning where the plants will go. As I stroll past the flowerbeds, trying to imagine them full of colour and shape, a strange memory from my childhood comes to mind. I'm walking with my father around the garden in Kent, discussing what he should plant in one of the borders when I suggest pampas grass. I had seen it in one of my friend's gardens and immediately fallen in love with its long willowy fronds that reminded me of sand dunes and beach holidays.

'There is absolutely no way I am having that awful plant here,' my father blurts out with unexpected passion. 'It's for swingers!' I look at him in total confusion.

Later, I ask my mother what a swinger is. As quick as flash, she retorts with her customary flare: 'It's a monkey, my love, who runs off with another monkey's banana, or, in this case, someone else's other half. A bit like Aunt Patricia.'

Utterly confused, I ask my enlightened friend, Jessica, if she knows what swingers are. 'You really don't know? It's when married couples shag each other.' After that, I never could look Aunt Patricia in the eye again, or for that matter, Mrs Wiley, who had the pampas grass growing in her front garden.

My basket is full of sweet-smelling bulbs: muscari, crocus, narcissus, hyacinth, tulip, aconite, English bluebell and allium. I'm hoping they will blossom into a magnificent pollinator hub for the price of a single potted shrub.

I feel like a detectorist digging for gold as I excavate the stony soil for my bulbs. The biggest are the allium "globemasters" which look like giant garlics and should grow into towering, saucer-shaped purple balls swarming with bees and other pollinators. I need to excavate a foot down for these. I have forgotten how backbreaking planting bulbs is, particularly when the earth is full of large pieces of chalk and you have fifty bulbs to bed down by the end of the day. But I try to keep the end result in mind – a glorious display next spring. I'm forced to use a naff floral kneeler which my mother gave me for Christmas last year, but I have to admit, it's doing a good job on my knees; they've only gone numb once.

Fortunately, the morning stays dry and I get the work completed sooner than I had anticipated. The final bulbs are the deep purple

Wildlife-Friendly Plants, Bulbs and Shrubs

MY SHOPPING LIST

Autumn-flowering

Pink/Violet	Sedum "Herbstfreude" (Autumn joy)
White	Aster "novi-belgii" (Michaelmas daisy)
Yellow	Helenium autumnale (Common sneezeweed)
Scented	Zaluzianskya ovata (Night-scented phlox)
Tubular	Origanum laevigatum "herrenhausen" (Sneezeweed)
Single/flat	Anemone "Honorine jobert" (Japanese anemone)
Bulbs	Cyclamen hederifolium (ivy-leaved) and crocus speciosus

Winter-flowering

Pink/Violet	Iris unguicularis (Algerian iris)
White	Garrya elliptica "James Roof" (silk tassel bush)
Yellow	Mahonia x media "Charity" and/or "japonica"
Scented	Viburnum x bodnantense "dawn"
Tubular	Helleborus foetidus (Stinking hellebore)
Single/flat	Choisya ternate (Mexican orange)
Bulbs	Arum italicum "marmoratum"

Shopping List Continued...

Spring-flowering

Pink/Violet	Ceanothus "Concha"
White	Magnolia "stellata"
Yellow	Forsythia "golden bells"
Scented	Philadelphus coronarius "Aureus" (Mock orange)
Tubular	Campanula "Kent belle" (Bellflower)
Single/flat	Vibernum opulus (Guelder rose)
Bulbs	Allium "globemaster", fritillaria, muscari, English bluebell, narcissus, tulip & hyacinth

Summer-flowering

Pink/Violet	Lavandula angustifolia (English lavender)
White	Hydrangea paniculata (Limelight hydrangea)
Yellow	Hypericum "Hidcote" (St John's Wort)
Scented	Nepeta "Purrsian blue" (Catmint)
Tubular	Digitalis purpurae (Foxglove)
Single/flat	Geranium "Rozanne" (Cranesbill)

Late Summer-flowering

Pink/violet	Buddleia "davidii" (Butterfly bush)
White	Phlox paniculata "White Admiral"
Yellow	Achillea "Moonshine"
Scented	Origanum vulgare "aureum" (Wild marjoram)
Tubular	Salvia nemorosa "Caradonna" (Woodland sage)
Single/flat	Echinacea "purpurae"

muscari that will be among the first spearheads to appear in spring. My father's terrace was covered in them when I was growing up and I always remember them smothered in bees. I put the remaining leftover bulbs into an empty terracotta pot and sprinkle in a few wildflower seeds just as my father would have done before going inside for a much-needed cup of tea and a tuna toastie. Georgie is licking her lips too. She's been keeping me company in the garden all morning, sniffing out mice and chasing pheasants, but it's time for her lunch and a snuggle!

FOURTEEN

LET'S TALK ABOUT
WORMS

The next morning, Ron comes round to help me rebuild our compost heap. Ed and I let the original one decay years ago; there didn't seem any point, at the time, keeping something that smelt rank and had sprouted fungi and ivy.

Unlike yesterday, the garden is damp and drizzly and eerily quiet except for the intermittent metallic ping of a raindrop or two falling off from the trees. Ron and I are both looking particularly scruffy. I was out late last night and woken early by Georgie barking at a squawking pheasant outside the back door, presumably squabbling with a competitor for the scraps I left out before going to bed. Ron is dressed in his signature scarecrow jacket tied up with string and a baggy pair of faded corduroy trousers tucked into his socks. He looks tired and drawn, bent over his fork, as he heaves the compounded mass of leaves, grass cuttings and garden debris that have accumulated in the old compost.

'You all right, Ron?' I ask eventually after going inside to make us both a reviving cup of strong coffee.

He nods but doesn't answer and then peers out from under his hat and winces slightly. I haven't seen him this quiet for ages. I leave him be, taking the wheelbarrow off into the garden to collect fresh leaves and see if I can find any suitable material for the compost. I'm resisting the urge to deadhead the faded flowers after Ron reminded me how important the seed heads are; they not only act as shelter for hibernating insects but are a vital food supply for birds, particularly finches, in winter. What I do find is a pile of grass cuttings by the fence which Ed left at the weekend after his last mow of the season. I shovel them into the wheelbarrow with a large spade, and potter mindlessly around the garden while Ron continues the hard work by the shed. He has cleared everything out of the wooden pen which our predecessors built for their composting needs several decades ago and revealed its three compartments – one for fresh cuttings, one for older cuttings and a third for leaves. Ron has kindly brought his hammer and nails over to strengthen the sides that, I notice, have collapsed.

'Is there anything you can't do?' I say when I return, hoping he has recovered a bit.

'What's that, dear?'

'Oh, nothing, Ron, I was just saying…' and then I break off, realising, yet again, he hasn't got his hearing aid turned up and is probably miles away.

I watch wistfully as he empties my leaves and grass into one of his newly excavated chambers and then reaches deep into his pocket for a plastic bag. It's filled with fruit and vegetable peelings, and he scatters them over the compost heap.

'The worms will love these,' he says, loudly, making both me and Georgie jump at the same time. He's looking across at us and smiling broadly. 'Go and get a watering can, would you, dear? We need to keep everything moist.'

I scuttle off, and when I return, he's sitting on an upturned log by our shed, eating a banana. I sit down beside him and he starts telling me all about worms and how important they are in maintaining healthy compost. I feel I'm back in biology class again at school or listening to my father giving a nature lesson.

'Did you know that if worms eat enough decomposing matter, they can poo the equivalent of their entire body weight in one day?' he says, laughing and throwing his banana skin over his shoulder into the compost.

'They're like worker ants in a nest, beavering away underground, doing all the dirty work for the benefit of us all.'

I love Ron's enthusiasm for the garden. He reminds me so much of my father and our special relationship, and I feel calm today, with him by my side.

'Well, dear, I hope Ed is happy with his new compost. I know the worms will be pleased and the garden spiders, centipedes, dormice and beetles. You might even get the odd hedgehog, snake or toad, if you're lucky. Tell him from me, he won't regret it.'

I thank him, and watch him return to his garden. One thing I'm sure of, Ed will be delighted with it when he realises that he doesn't need to buy fertiliser anymore and has a handy, home-spun recycling unit.

I walk down to the village with Georgie after lunch and pass a tatty garden on the hill which has been left to naturalise with its surroundings. There are no formal borders, neat edges or pristine lawn. The grass has been left to grow long, and the weeds, ivy and nettles have multiplied everywhere. There's a small pond on the terrace attracting flies and wasps and a compost heap against the fence, just like Ron's.

A year ago, I would have turned my nose up at this messy garden but with my new enlightened hat on, I'm judging it differently today. I can see it is doing more to boost biodiversity than my neat and tidy space ever could, and the owners have put nature first. It's not beautiful or stylish but there's a sense of harmony and calm about it which I hadn't noticed before.

Continuing my walk, I mull over the question that has been nagging me for days. How can a nation of gardeners with over twenty-three million private gardens (a land mass of one and a half times the size of Wales) end up being one of the most nature-depleted places in the world? How can that even happen?

I'm still struggling to comprehend it when I arrive back at the house. Eager to get to the bottom of my conundrum, I start googling the history of gardening in the UK, and what I discover surprises me. It also helps explain, to a large degree, how tradition and fashion have shaped our current attitudes to gardening and how poor decision-making in the last two to three hundred years have got us into the biodiversity mess we are in today.

Prior to the Industrial Revolution, with the exception of a few stately homes, formal gardens didn't exist at all. Before the expansion of cities and towns, Britain was largely made up of small, rural hamlets and any outside space was shared by the villagers. Their gardens were the meadows, the village greens and the fields, and before the advent of the car, the countryside was bound together by animal tracks, footpaths and bridle ways.

But as urban development increased, so did the desire for private, outside space and gardening became more popular. By the mid-nineteenth century, it had become a fashionable hobby and wealthy tradesmen returning from the Empire came laden with exciting new plants and trees to sell to wealthy Victorians, keen to show off their exotic gardens.

Unfortunately, these foreign plants often brought disease and could be invasive, crowding out our native plants. At the same time, non-native birds, animals and insects were being shipped in as "curiosities" for wealthy landowners and collectors, wreaking havoc on our native wildlife. Grey squirrels are an example of an imported species which has slowly decimated our native red squirrel population. There are now fewer than 140,000 red squirrels in the UK compared to over 2.5 million greys, and only a few remote areas in Britain where they can be spotted.

The real harm to wildlife, though, came after the Second World War when farmers and homeowners were encouraged to grow more vegetables to help feed a hungry nation. What happened in the wider countryside with the removal of woods and hedgerows to create more space for arable fields was mirrored in people's gardens. Many were dug up for vegetable patches and traditional native plant species and vital wildlife habitats like ponds, trees and hedges were lost. Gardens simply got tidied up, and to do this quickly and effectively, the British gardener turned to a new, ingenious invention – weedkiller – and other harmful chemicals that are toxic to wildlife.

By the 1980s, the unruly but diverse English cottage garden was on the wane, and the new fashion was contemporary neatness and order. Gardens were seen as an extension of the house as opposed to the countryside and wildness was no longer tolerated. Everyone wanted a manicured lawn with clean edges and neat, manageable flowerbeds. Native plants went out of fashion and were replaced with exotic, sculptural species like bonsai, phormium and canna lily, which were striking but had very little wildlife value. The impact of all these changes was devastating for nature.

If I knew earlier what I know today about the dire state of our natural world, I hope I would have acted differently in my own garden, but all this is pointless speculation and counterproductive. What's important *now* is how quickly I can change. I owe that much to myself as well as to my father. I know Dad would want me to return to my roots and to nature; he always believed I would. I simply need to let go of the guilt, step up a gear and put my foot firmly down on the accelerator.

FIFTEEN

NOT IVY!

This morning, the garden is clothed in a light mist and the sun is strobing through the haze, turning the dew drops on the rowan tree into festive sparkles. I'm sitting at my bedroom window thinking about my next task in the garden and admiring the light display. While I sit and stare, four or five blackbirds descend from nowhere and take up positions on one of the branches where clusters of small berries hang like ivory grapes. One by one, they pull the fruits apart like ravenous raptors before flying off into the mist again, their appetites replete after their breakfast feast. A few moments later, a robin hops out from under a bush and starts scooping up the juicy off-cuts that have fallen onto the grass, before being frightened off by a lugubrious wood pigeon who has weighed in.

Looking across the front garden, I see the lawn has turned overnight into a massive multicoloured puzzle of autumn leaves. Winter is just around the corner and for the first time in years

I'm excited by the changing seasons. I feel a warm glow inside, and I know I am on the right track.

Later that day, my head is swimming with the carol, *The Holly and the Ivy,* as I sweep up the autumn leaves on the drive, making neat piles like Ron would do, before dumping them on his new swish compost. I've just ordered three ready-made ivy screens to cover a rather unattractive wall on our south-facing terrace. They're the evergreen native variety – hedera helix – which Ron recommends and should produce some lovely flowers and berries for the birds and pollinators to feed off this winter.

My mother is not impressed. She's come for the day and I'm showing her around the garden, explaining my plans for boosting wildlife.

'Not ivy! It's a terrible nuisance and will spread everywhere, ruin your house with its clingy roots and look a complete mess after a few years. Why don't you plant a climbing hydrangea, like the one we had in Kent, or a pretty honeysuckle?' she says in her inimitable way. At eighty-three, my mother hasn't lost any of her zest or obsession with order and style and whether she means to or not, she retains a remarkable ability to shrink my enthusiasm for anything outside her narrow sphere of what's acceptable, in a matter of seconds. Even when I fight back, as now, and try to convince her of the benefits of ivy, she remains annoyingly resistant.

'I'm sure the bees and butterflies would prefer to forage for their late-summer nectar in a much prettier plant, and anyway, your father was always going on about the wonders of honeysuckle and climbing hydrangea. Didn't you once find a rare butterfly in the honeysuckle by the garage?'

I did – a white admiral – but that wasn't going to change my mind. The screens had been ordered (at some expense) and I wasn't going to cancel them just to please my mother; she would have to suck it up this time.

She's more encouraging about the shrubs that I've planted in my new wildlife border. 'That's more like it, darling,' she says, as I point out the philadelphus and buddleia "davidii" in the front bed. Both shrubs are looking perky and green among the sterile mass of desiccated hydrangeas and phormiums.

I decided at the start of the project that I wouldn't rip out any of my old plants, however insignificant their value to wildlife. I didn't want to create large gaps everywhere which I would need to refill. My approach was always to add to what I already had and restore diversity that way. Evolution rather than revolution.

She smiles approvingly when she sees my new sedum, geranium "Rozanne" and white hebe and is noticeably impressed with the white and pink Japanese anemones that Ron recently transferred from his garden.

'A touch of the exotic at last,' she says, teasingly. 'I'm glad to see you haven't gone completely native.'

Returning to the house, we chat about the flowers I want to plant in the spring – aster, verbena, helenium, origanum, echinacea, pinks, nepeta and English lavender. She can sense my excitement and, by the time we reach Ron's spectacular compost heap, both our moods have visibly lifted.

'Now that's what I would call a proper compost,' she says animatedly, staring at Ron's creation. I can see his banana skin is still lying on top of the mound and nicely decomposing with his other fruit peelings.

We laugh together, remembering my father's unwieldy pile of decomposing matter at the back of the garage that got complaints from the Blakemores for attracting rats and other vermin, and left an unbearable stench in the garden. The smell became so potent in summer that it would make us all retch.

'Did you know we actually fell out completely with the Blakemores over that wretched compost?' my mother reflects. 'They stopped talking to us when your father refused to clear it up, despite the unbearable smell. Timmy really was a stubborn old fart, sometimes, and what with the compost and rabbit fiasco, we weren't the most popular family in the neighbourhood.'

We end our walk with a quick look where the new trees are going in a fortnight and a visit to the insect hotel. I want to see if it's attracted any visitors.

'What am I supposed to be looking at?' my mother remarks discouragingly as she peers awkwardly into the mass of cobwebs, moss and corrugated cardboard. 'Forgive me for saying this, but it looks like something you might have made in Kindergarten and it seems a bit empty.'

She must have seen my expression wilt because she quickly and affectionately nudges me, pecks my cheek with her ruby lips and says with a twinkle in her eye: 'Ah, well, my darling, perhaps your insects prefer the seaside. You could try adding sand.'

The ridiculous thought makes us both burst out laughing.

SIXTEEN

TREE THERAPY

The oak is the largest and longest-lived of our native trees and a very familiar object in most parts of the British Isles. The human centenarian is regarded with reverence... and (when) we think of the long period of history of which he has been a spectator, (or even) active maker, the huge oak has probably lived through ten or twenty such periods. Compared with the oak, man is but of mushroom growth. It does not produce an acorn until sixty or seventy years old and even then, is not mature. Not till a century and a half have passed over its head is its timber fit for use.

I'm lying under our ancient oak at the bottom of our garden where the rabbits like to sit, reading my 1938 *Observer's Book of Trees and Shrubs*; I'm trying to imagine how this massive tree began its life and what it has witnessed over five long centuries. It's awkward reading on my back and I have to keep putting the book down to rest my arms, but this gives me an opportunity to examine the tree in more detail. Looking up through the thick spider's web of branches with their green and bronze-stained leaves shimmering in the breeze, I can see the red-hot poker sun trying to penetrate through. It's as if the oak is resisting its rays, protecting me from the scorching heat and allowing me to wallow in the cool shadows of its voluminous cape.

Our oak is over 100 feet high and so densely packed with mid-summer foliage that it would take a meteor fireball to reach me. My eyes close, and for the brief moment I'm still conscious, it's just me, the oak and the gentle sound of rustling leaves. My eyes close and I'm lulled into a deep reverie.

I'm back in the hunting grounds of Penshurst Place where Dad and I walked this morning, standing under one of the oldest oak trees in Britain – the "Bear Oak", as it is locally known. This colossus of a tree is over a thousand years old and has more history written into its deeply furrowed bark than all the other trees in the park.

Legend has it that Henry VIII, who owned Penshurst Place in 1521, wooed his second wife, Anne Boleyn, under its leafy canopy and, many years later, their daughter, Elizabeth, would rest under the oak during her stays at the fourteenth-century manor.

I try to step inside the massive trunk which has split in half and hollowed out with age, but my father stops me. He's afraid I will disturb the fragile ecosystem of the tree.

'There will be over 2,500 living creatures in this one oak,' he says as I poke my finger through the deep grooves of the bark. 'Hundreds of insects will be doing exactly what you are doing with your finger – burrowing into the bark – as they search for temporary shelter, and owls, woodpeckers and nuthatches may well be nesting in the hollow trunk. Some of our rarest butterflies will lay their eggs in the oak and even the moss and lichen that grows on the branches is an important food source for insects and birds.'

I'm disappointed I can't get closer to this veteran of the forest. I would like to imagine myself back in Tudor England, but I've learnt many things today, and I know one thing for sure – I will never walk past another oak without remembering the great "Bear" of Penshurst and the thousands of organisms living inside.

Today, I'm laying the foundations of a new woodland and hedgerow along the stretch of grass where Ron and I erected the bird box over four months ago.

The birds seem as excited as I am, tweeting loudly and merrily as I make my way down the grassy strip, waiting for the influx of trucks and men bringing my fifty saplings.

It's a lovely sunny morning and strobes of bright light are streaming through the bare branches of the trees, accentuating their shape and giving the garden a majestic, heavenly appeal.

The men from the nursery come powering up the drive on the dot of eight o'clock, and I can see the saplings piled high in the back of their jeeps like bound prisoners being taken to a new location. I can hardly believe my wood is about to begin. It's been a dream of mine ever since Ron sowed the idea in October and although it's my most expensive wilding project to date, I know the benefits to our garden and, more importantly, our wildlife, will far outweigh the cost.

I've chosen all the tree species that Ron recommended – birch, beech, pine, larch and sorbus – but I've also added a few of my own – an English oak, in memory of my father, a liquidambar, Rockhampton red and tulip tree. I saw the last three displayed at Kew Gardens on a recent visit to London and was immediately swept away by their tantalising autumn hue.

All the saplings, even the specimen varieties, have been grown in the UK, and seeing them lined up on the drive with their large Union Jack labels proudly displayed around their trunks, they look like an eclectic band of British soldiers.

After bringing the men a tray of coffee and biscuits, I sit on a log and chat to Chris, the manager, about my wildlife project and my dreams of restoring the woodland habitats. I tell him that I want to rewild the entire grass avenue where the new trees are going, and make it into a peaceful sanctuary where the family can stroll and be at one with nature.

'I think it's a great idea,' he says approvingly. 'We should all be planting more trees to make up for the billions that we cut down globally each year. It terrifies me to think of all the ancient woodland we're losing.'

He goes on to explain how our forests are the lungs of the world, containing three quarters of the world's plants and animals. 'Without them we will struggle to stop our planet overheating,' he said, staring forlornly out at the new trees. 'Of course, it will take decades before your new saplings reach full maturity and start absorbing carbon dioxide from the atmosphere, but it's a start.'

While we've been talking, the men have taken the saplings down the garden and are starting to dig out large square holes.

'My cue to join them,' says Chris, jumping up. 'Thanks for the coffee.'

He strolls off and I sit back and lean my head back against the larch, savouring the sappy aroma and warming my face in the sun. I start to feel panic rise again in the muscles of my head and the fear that maybe I've left my tree project too late to make any difference. I shut my eyes and start concentrating on my breathing, hoping that the meditation will relax me.

I'm distracted by Georgie who has ripped the felt off her tennis ball and is popping it in her mouth like a piece of bubble gum. At least one of us is oblivious to the climate crisis, I think to myself, cheering up immediately. She's got half an eye on a pair of sprightly squirrels chasing each other up and down a scaly larch trunk like kids in a playground. Occasionally, one slips and then slides down the totem pole trunk like a lump of wet paint before resuming the precipitous climb all over again.

'Watch out for those squirrels,' Chris hollers from across the garden. 'They'll strip the bark off your new trees if you let them and steal the birds' eggs in the spring. Bloody pests, they are these days.'

I nod in agreement. Our greys seem very different from the red squirrels I remember from my childhood, much more predatory and always hogging the bird feeders. The other day, I saw a particularly cheeky one removing the lid off the nut feeder and squeezing its head right down the wire tube to reach the compacted nuts. Nearby, the birds watched helplessly as their breakfast was gobbled up in front of them.

After the recent heavy rain, the ground is soft and moist and the men work quickly. They get the first tranche of trees – the beech, tulip, oak and larch – planted and staked in under an hour, and by lunch, all the silver birch and pine are also in position. I can see my woodland taking shape before my very eyes. Having some evergreen varieties adds welcome colour and will give the birds and small mammals somewhere to hide in winter when the autumn gales have stripped the other trees of their summer foliage.

The final job of the day is to plant the new hedge saplings. While the men set about digging holes for the holly, yew and beech I have chosen to replace what we ripped out of the garden twenty years ago, I plant daffodil bulbs, English bluebell and snake's-head fritillary in an open, sunny area. Next year, I will add foxgloves, ferns, cuckoo pint, wild garlic and lesser celandine and complete a bona fide woodland glade. My wildlife gardening guide describes a woodland glade as a vital wildflower meadow for our flora and fauna, sustaining over twenty butterfly species. If I'm lucky, I might get to glimpse a speckled wood, a comma, or even a white admiral or purple emperor butterfly exploring the luxuriant undergrowth.

Later, after the men have packed up and gone, I'm admiring my new stretch of woodland when I notice the insect hotel has been completely dismantled by a large animal, most likely Georgie. There's a gaping hole in the top floor, as if a missile has struck the roof, and sticks, moss, matting and bamboo strewn all over the grass. I will have to strengthen the hotel's defences if I want to safeguard future residents.

'Well, darling, it's not my style but your father would love it,' my mother says, looking at the lawn which hasn't been cut for weeks. The grass is about a foot high and there are patches of brown where the leaves have decomposed.

'You haven't changed; you are so like your father,' she says resignedly, wiping the moisture and muck off her shoes.

We walk silently back to the house together. It's strange she feels I haven't changed. I certainly feel I have and not for the better sometimes, but then, when I think about it, perhaps she's right. Perhaps I'm not *so* different after all. Perhaps the child in me is still alive; she just went underground for forty years.

Later, we're sitting at the kitchen table reminiscing about my father and the family home when Mum suddenly blurts out: 'Roses!' I nearly jump out of my seat. 'Your father loved roses. I knew you were missing something. Unless I'm very much mistaken, your new garden doesn't have any.'

She's right, of course, I've completely overlooked my father's favourite flower. He worshipped the rose. It was as much his emblem as our nation's, and the bedrock of our English country garden in the 1970s. Throughout the summer months, he would spend hours immersed in his old hybrid and wild rose bushes, cultivating and constantly improving his favourites while religiously recording the wildlife that visited the resplendent blooms. I can see him now, surrounded by the tall colourful blossoms, chatting to me happily as we both infused the roses' potent scents, and, for a brief moment, I'm back there, in my childhood garden, with my beloved father. The warm memory stirs a tingling in my blood and, without delay, I dig out all his old rose manuals from the school chest, including his most recent – *The New Rose Expert* by Dr D. G. Hessayon – and start compiling a list of the varieties I know my father would have approved of.

Like flowers in general, I discover that the most wildlife-friendly roses have single or open blooms that are easily accessible to pollinators.

The more tightly bound the petal arrangement, as with floribunda, the harder it is for the insects to reach in for the nectar and pollen, unless they have very long tongues. I also learn that roses with arching stems and dense foliage are popular with nesting birds, while scented roses and those that produce hips in autumn, are most attractive to butterflies and moths as well as other insects and birds.

I decide my best bet, to avoid an argument with my mother, is to list two of her favourite floribundas – rosa "Arthur Bell" and rosa "Queen Elizabeth" – which she remembers buying in the 1970s, and then add a rosa rugosa "Alba" (white) and rosa rugosa "Scabrosa" (dark pink) to the list. I also include two scented ramblers that I know my father grew up the side of the house – "Rambling Rector" and "Frances E. Lester". Both are rich in nectar and pollen and offer juicy rose hips in autumn which the birds will love. Knowing the cheaper, bare-rooted varieties are only available in winter, I quickly scan the internet and find what I am after on the David Austin website. The Shropshire nursery has been synonymous with English roses for as long as I can remember.

The English rose, the "Queen of Flowers", is, in fact, not native to Britain; it was brought to England over two thousand years ago by the Romans who, like my father, adored and revered the gorgeous blooms. They would scatter rose petals on the floor of their villas or on their beds before making love, believing them to enhance fertility.

When I tell my mother this, she laughs and says in characteristically stiff-upper-lip fashion: 'Typical Italians. Always obsessed with sex.'

SEVENTEEN

POND DIGGING

Dad and I are together in the Victorian greenhouse. It's a balmy August afternoon in 1978 and we are potting seeds for his vegetable garden. He suddenly stops what he is doing and looks up and I notice a shadow of sadness has passed over his eyes. 'Your mother wants a tennis court,' he says sombrely. 'She thinks it would be great for the family and would mean you and Simon could invite your friends over for tennis and tea.'

He waits for my reaction, but I am speechless.

'It means getting rid of all this,' he continues, waving his arms in a giant arc. 'It would mean digging out the orchard, removing all the wild borders and wildflowers and churning up our little wildlife meadow. It would mean no more dens in the bushes by the garage or apples in the autumn. The garden would look very different.'

'I think you should refuse,' I reply defiantly. 'I don't want a tennis court. Who plays tennis anyway? I like the garden just as it is.'

I didn't realise it then, but my mother and father had been wrangling for weeks over the plan. My mother loved tennis, and felt our garden had become too wild and unkempt and almost impossible to manage. It was also the era of Virginia Wade and Bjorn Borg and she secretly harboured dreams of at least one of her children becoming a future Wimbledon champion. The fact that Simon was stuck at boarding school for most of the year and I had no desire to learn tennis didn't stop her dreaming.

In the end, my father succumbed to Mum's quiet persuasion. He could see how uncomfortable she was in the existing garden, particularly when they had friends around and she would have to wade through nettles and long grass to reach the deckchairs. She persuaded him with her flamboyant landscaping plans for the tennis court which she said would far outshine anything they had so far done in the garden.

Three years later, the court was built and by then I didn't care. I was a teenager and rapidly losing interest in the garden and nature. I was spending less time with Dad in general and rarely volunteered to help him with the wildlife. My new priorities were sport, parties and boys.

My mother was true to her word. She created some magnificent borders around the side of the court and replaced the apple trees with a number of ornamental fruit trees. Although it was never the same wildlife garden, it did evolve into something beautiful, and my father ensured it never lost its diversity, scent and colour.

I haven't told Ed yet, but I'm siting our new pond in the middle of his bonfire. It's by far the best position – sunny and away from the trees, so should stay clear of leaves and remain relatively algae-free.

Ed isn't pleased though. 'I admit I'm not Monty Don or Alan Titchmarsh but you know how much I enjoy a bonfire,' he says, trying to change my mind. 'Anyway, what will we do with all the leaves and branches – chuck them into Ron's garden?'

'We'll compost them with all the other debris or use them to make homes for the wildlife,' I say a little too enthusiastically. He looks crestfallen. 'You wait, it will be great,' I persist. 'We'll likely get fish, frogs, newts and toads, just like we did when the children were small. In fact, the pond could be a magnet for so many creatures – foxes, hedgehogs, dragonflies, hoverflies, even lizards.

Ed isn't convinced. I'm beginning to sound like my father and I can see Ed's eyes glazing over. He senses, though, he's on a losing wicket and leaves me to get on with my planning.

Scouring the internet for garden pond facts, I'm horrified to discover that nearly seventy per cent (600,000) of farm and garden ponds have disappeared from the UK countryside since the beginning of the nineteenth century. Although much of this decline is due to farmers wanting more space, homeowners, like us, have also played a part. When garden ponds went out of fashion in the 1970s and '80s, many were destroyed or simply left to dry out. Our obsession with health and safety hasn't helped either and, though I hate to admit it now, I'm as guilty as the next person. My natural instinct when I discovered our pond back in 2002 was to get rid of it. I was convinced one of the children would drown or get some rat-born disease from swallowing the water. So rather than make it safe by fencing it off, I took the coward's way out and drained it.

I never thought for one moment about the wildlife I was destroying in the process and the knock-on effect this would have on the garden's fragile ecosystem.

Ron has come around to help me install the pond, the last of my wilding manifesto tasks for this year. I've bought a giant plastic preformed monstrosity off the internet which looks like a wonky paddling pool, and it's been blocking out the sun in Ed's study for weeks, reminding him of the imminent demise of his bonfire.

Ron waits patiently outside the front door as I put my boots on and then helps me carry the pond down to the meadow. Our journey is slow and sombre like a funeral march, and anyone watching would be forgiven for thinking we were carrying a large black coffin down to the cemetery.

I notice from behind that he's looking strained and older than he did when we were working together on the compost. Something's not right but I can't put my finger on it. Even Georgie has noticed and is trying to liven him up by constantly pressing her nose into his jacket.

'You all right, Ron?' I call out tentatively as we march slowly through the long grass, but he doesn't reply.

We lay the structure down on the grass, and he leans over to measure it with a long piece of string. I notice him wince as if in pain and then rub his forehead. His neuralgia is obviously back, and I'm concerned about the digging he's about to do.

'Look Ron, if this is too much...'

He interrupts abruptly: 'I'm fine dear, really. Please don't worry about me. I want to help.' He looks up at me as he says this, tips his hat and smiles, and I relax a little.

Fortunately, the soil is really soft after decades of bonfires and Ron's spade slices through it easily. It takes him no time at all to dig a large square trench deep enough for the pond.

While he excavates, I pile up the stones and charcoal released from the ash. The fire debris will make an attractive surround for the pond. I also set aside clumps of dead nettle, grass and green alkanet to replant later.

Ron lets out a long sigh when he finally finishes digging the metre-wide hole. Rivulets of sweat are running off his brow and I'm hoping he will stop and take a rest, but he presses on regardless, infilling the hole methodically until the last bit of soil has been replaced.

'I'll make us a cup of tea,' I say at last.

'I'm all right, love. I'll get this finished first.'

I'm touched he wants to help. Over the last few months, we've become close and I'm not sure I could have done the wilding project without him.

I'm hoping he's enjoyed my company as much as I have appreciated his and it has relieved the solitude of living alone. He once told me how loneliness follows him around the house like a shadow, since his wife died, and haunts him in his bed at night. 'Enjoy being young, dear,' he said. 'Old age creeps up on you like a cancer and, before you know it, you're too doddery to enjoy the things you once did.'

I hope my wildlife project has helped reignite some of Ron's past pleasures and given him, like it has me, an extra special reason to get up in the morning.

It's nearly midday and the sun has gone behind the clouds. It's noticeably cooler as I walk back to the house to get a jacket. When I return to the meadow, I find Ron hunched over our garden table, mumbling to himself and mopping his brow with a large white hankie. I rush over and, hearing me, he looks up and forces a smile.

'I'm all right, love. You just need to fill the pond now with rainwater. The tap water has nasty chemicals in it so use the water from the butt. You can use mine if you don't have enough.'

I return for the water and Ron goes back to his garden to find some large slabs of chalky stone to place around the side of the pond. The stone makes the finished pond look remarkably authentic; it could be a natural feature which has been in the garden for years. I'm delighted and, after the final slab is laid and the pond filled with water, we both sit down under a large willow my father planted when we moved here and silently admire the new creation. The light is being to fade and the shadows are lengthening across the garden and, by the time we finally get up to make our way back to the house, the trees have been lost in darkness. Ron points out a flock of black gulls that are flying in unison like a squadron of spitfires across the dusky sky.

'They're flying home to roost dear, after spending the day in the ploughed fields behind the house. Heading home for shut-eye just like I'll be doing soon,' he says with a wink. I laugh, thankful that he has recovered his spirit.

The next day, he knocks on my door early. He's looking tired again, but he has something in his hand which he wants to show me. As he unfolds his palm, I see he's holding a tiny silver dog no bigger than a two pence piece. 'It's for you, dear. I know how much you like dogs and it was something I found in my garden years ago, cleaned it up and then forgot about it. It's been on my shelf in the garage waiting to be re-homed.'

I'm so touched, I'm lost for words but before I can thank him, he's tipped his hat and walked away.

That was the last time I saw dear Ron. He died suddenly two weeks later when Ed and I were away in Scotland and I never got to say goodbye. I should have chased after him that day and given him a big hug, I should have told him how much the family loved him and I should have thanked him for everything he had done for me over the years. But I didn't, and his passing broke my spirit for a while. His legacy was my garden; the wildlife garden we started and completed together and all the hope it now represents.

EIGHTEEN
REGENERATION

One month is past, another is begun,
Since merry bells rang out the dying year
And buds of rarest green began to peer,
As if impatient for a warmer sun;
And though the distant hills are bleak and dun,
The virgin snowdrop, like a lambent fire,
Pierces the cold earth with it's green-streaked spire
And in dark woods, the wandering little one,
May find a primrose.
Hartley Coleridge

WINTER

1 February

There's an amazing red-rose sunrise this morning and the larch by our garage has turned amber. I rush outside to take a photograph and stand in awe as a pair of goldfinches emerge from the high branches and undulate playfully, their striking yellow-black wings sparkling in the early morning sunlight. I think immediately of Ron and how he used to stand at his kitchen window watching the goldfinches flock to his feeders and how, each autumn, migrating thrushes, fieldfares, chaffinches and redwings would descend on his garden to feast on the fruits of his apple and rowan trees. And now the goldfinches are nesting in my garden, feasting on my niger seeds and singing for me. It's been four years since my wilding project began and hardly a day goes by now when I'm not treated to some new natural phenomenon or uplifting display.

I used to dread the cold, featureless months of January and February and almost never ventured into the garden other than for a walk or to collect firewood. But now I'm out every day, dressed in my voluminous trousers, rain hat and heavy boots, eager to glimpse any new sign of wildlife. Georgie is eager to be out too, drawn by the abundance of new smells and wild havens hiding intriguing creatures great and small.

I can't believe how far I have come in just a sprinkling of time. Returning the garden to nature has helped me reconnect with my roots in a way I never thought possible a few years ago, and this connection, this intangible pull from the past, has somehow given me hope and inner peace as well as a reason to get up in the morning. I feel rooted again, close to my father again and with nature at the forefront of everything I do. I feel this journey of mine, this natural odyssey, is only just beginning, though. In reflective moments, I imagine my father looking down at me from his celestial arbour and smiling, proud of what I've achieved and glad that I'm on track again with wildlife gardening. He would, of course, be urging me to do more. I can hear his plea constantly echoing in my thoughts, repeated over and over, no longer occasioning guilt, but inspiring me on: *'Never lose the child inside you, Annabel, and never forget that nature brings enduring peace and happiness.'* I keep his letter tucked inside the one book that still has the power to move me to tears – his precious *Natural History of British Butterflies* which rests in pride of place on my bedside table. I often reread its heartfelt message when I feel the need to be close to him again.

My father's old field glasses have come in very useful too, particularly for spotting birds. The best time to see the birds is early in the morning when they are most active at the feeders. Today, I was "twitching" at 7.30 a.m. and saw a conveyor belt of robin, nuthatch, greater spotted woodpecker, brambling, blackcap, long-tailed tit, great tit, chaffinch, pheasant and the ubiquitous wood pigeon – flitting from one feeder to the other in a grab-and-snack style skirmish before being scared off by a menacing magpie or jackdaw.

I had my glasses fixed on this captivating display of avian hierarchy when I noticed three or four thrush-like birds pecking on the ground under the old apple tree. Zooming in, I saw they were fieldfares enjoying the soggy remains of last autumn's windfalls. Like their redwing cousins, fieldfares are migrant birds arriving in the UK every autumn from Scandinavia to savour our rich supply of seeds and berries. It feels momentous seeing them in the garden for the first time; a milestone reached.

I wonder what other birds might have migrated from the northern hemisphere to over-winter in the garden while their fair-weather cousins remain thousands of miles away. What birds achieve by crossing three continents to reach winter breeding or feeding grounds, is little short of a miracle, particularly since their journey is thwart with danger.

2 February

The mercury has plunged overnight, and a heavy frost has turned the garden shrubs and trees into ice-statues. Icicles hang like silvery arrowheads from the roof of the house and garage, while our bedroom windows have become frosted fern etchings. I can't remember it being this cold since my childhood.

The crisp air feels like a knife edge on my cheeks as I step outside with Georgie and scrunch my way down to the new wildflower meadow, the one I created with Ron. I'm erecting a new trail camera to discover what animal has taken up residence in a pile of sticks and leaves the other side of the fence. I attach the camera to the chicken wire, switch it to "images" and then return to the back garden to replenish the bird feeders and remove the ice from the bird bath. A friendly robin hops down from the pear tree to say hello. I throw him some seeds and then, out of the corner of my eye, see Winston, my new friend. Winston is a tiny wren who lives on the terrace under one of the large terracotta pots, and he's discovered the thick roots of the wild geranium "edressi" I planted a year ago which is perfect for hiding in. When he's not foraging for spiders, grubs and seeds in the undergrowth, I often see him by the back door scooping up the crumbs I've thrown down. Winston might be the smallest bird in the garden but he lives up to his namesake in terms of both courage and ingenuity.

15 February

Another frosty February morning but the birds seem impervious to the cold. They have been serenading me happily since dawn and are enjoying the food I put out for them yesterday. The blackbird and robin are always the first to sing in the morning, their large orb eyes more adept at sensing the aurora light. I wonder if this is true of humans.

Accompanied by Georgie, I head out to check on my trail camera. I can't wait to see if it has captured any images overnight. It has; a hazy shot of a long, thin animal, presumably a stoat or weasel. That would make sense; all the poor rabbits have disappeared from the garden in recent months.

Georgie makes chase after our neighbour's cat. The poor feline finds itself constantly trapped in our garden these days and pursued by Georgie after discovering the holes which Ron and I cut for the hedgehogs.

I'm constantly reminded of Ron when I'm in my new wildlife garden. I miss his company more than I ever imagined I would, his dry humour and succinct but wise, warm words. Nothing will replace his presence next door and, each day, I'm met with emptiness and shadow where once we chatted happily over the garden gate or by the fence and where he used to tip his hat in friendly greeting. I can imagine what he would be saying to me now as I carefully drop the trespassing cat over our still-surviving dead hedge and back into the safety of its own garden: He would be saying: 'Still not got that bloody dog under control, dear. Well, it's a good thing it's a cat she's chasing and not a pheasant!'

1 March

Walking back from the village early this morning, I stop for a breather at the top of the steep chalk escarpment near our cottage and look back down the valley. The curved scrubland is still and stark and monotone in the dull light. The only sound is the occasional whoosh of a car going up the hill. The wintery landscape is devoid of vegetation and colour, and it makes me wonder if this is what our world would look like permanently if wildlife no longer existed.

Returning home, I sit at the open fire warming my toes while Georgie rests her head on my lap. I've found an anthology of poems that came over in my father's trunk which, if my memory serves me rightly, was a present from Dad when I left home to study English Literature at St Andrews University in 1984. Among the many "romantic" poems is Wordsworth's *Daffodils*; Keats's *Ode to Autumn*; Hardy's *The Darkling Thrush* and Clare's

February. They somehow seem more richly evocative of nature and more pertinent than they did when I first read them in the college library over three decades ago.

> *The hedgehog, from his hollow root,*
> *Sees the wood-moss clear of snow,*
> *And hunts the hedge for fallen fruit –*
> *Crab, hip, and winter-bitten sloe;*
> *But often checked by sudden fears,*
> *As shepherd-dog his haunt espies*
> *He rolls up in a ball of spears,*
> *And all his barking rage defies.*

The Romantics were writing in the early nineteenth century, around the time of the Industrial Revolution, and their laments about nature reflected their fears that rural life was being swallowed up by development and industrialisation. Reading the poems again reminds me that 200 years on, nature is still reeling from the impact of industrialisation, but is faced with even greater threats.

5 March

I'm in the garden, nearing dusk, when I find a solitary bee has taken up residence in one of the corrugated cardboard tubes inside my reconstructed insect hotel. It's most likely a hibernating mason or leafcutter bee as I notice the hole has been sealed up with what looks like dried leaves or rose petals. Lifting the earthy cardboard tube out gently, I disturb a large spider and a family of woodlice that have cocooned themselves in the warm winter shelter. The undersides of the tube are white with lichen, and as I gently replace it, my eye catches a large, leathery brown pupa sticking out of the soil. I take a quick photo and then make a hasty retreat before my intrusion wakes the moth or butterfly from its winter sleep. I discover later it was probably an angle shade moth chrysalis.

I stay in the garden, marvelling at the Neapolitan sunset as it turns from pastel pink, blue and yellow to light grey. The sky is streaked with thin white smoke trails from passing airplanes. As the colours fade, our tall trees are thrown into silhouette against the darkening sky and a hazy half-moon rises and appears above. I'm reminded of a balmy night last April when I saw my first hedgehog close-up in the garden. I was quietly resting on a bench admiring the sunset when I picked up a faint rustling in the long grass by the boundary. Sitting completely still, I waited and then a few seconds later I glimpsed a prickly mass out of the corner of my eye, about the size of a football, reflected in the fading light. I turned my head but the tiny beast had retreated back into the undergrowth and disappeared. I felt the same sense of awe that I felt with my father all those years ago when, as a young girl, I discovered the fox nestled in the straw at the back of our garage.

15 March

Stepping out into the bright morning sunshine, I notice the front borders have lost their winter drabness and turned, overnight it seems, into a carpet of fresh green growth. The bulbs that I planted so lovingly four years ago are finally emerging through the dead undergrowth, bringing unexpected but much-needed colour to the garden. They're all there – snowdrops, narcissi, tulips, muscari, crocuses and hyacinths – sweet arbiters of spring with the promise of rich nectar for our early pollinators.

I come across the first aconites of the year peeping up through the dead growth like a crowd of miniature courtiers with yellow heads and green ruffled collars and, all of a sudden, an enormous bumblebee lands on one of the brightest blooms, and I can almost sense its relief as it sinks its long tongue into the rich, welcoming flowerhead and sucks up the nectar. It's taken a year or two but, at last, my winter garden is blooming.

The honeyed winter honeysuckle on the south-facing wall is attracting a variety of flies and other insects and as I press my nose into it, I'm struck by the power of its scent. Like a familiar song from my youth, the aroma reignites memories, transporting me back in time to my childhood garden.

Our Kent honeysuckle is entwined around the bramble on the garage and spreading to the beech hedge, forming an archway which I can walk under. If I stand on tiptoe, I can smell the sweet scent of the creamy-yellow flowers; they hang like miniature lampshades and are covered in black insects.

I watch as a rare butterfly lands on a perfect bloom, rare because I have never seen this particular species in the garden before. It is quite large with splayed, jet-black and white wings. I rush off to find Dad and, when he sees the butterfly, he is as excited as I am by the discovery.

'That's a really special one. Well done for spotting such a beauty. It's a white admiral butterfly and it absolutely adores honeysuckle.'

He then explains that the larva will feed on the leaves and then curl up into a little silvery ball for the winter before emerging as a new butterfly in the spring. 'How's that for a little miracle of nature?' he says, staring down at me.

He takes my hand and we stand together silently watching the young butterfly as it suns itself on the flower. A sudden rustle in the beech hedge disturbs our peace and the magical butterfly rises up and floats away like a large black feather on the breeze, before disappearing into our neighbour's garden, never to be seen again.

16 March

A nuthatch is monopolising the sunflower seeds this morning. It keeps sneaking off to the silver birch in our back garden to crack open the shell and release the kernel against the trunk. As I focus the field glasses, my eye is drawn to a slither of movement on the birch. It's a short-toed treecreeper, the first I've spotted this winter in the garden, and it's shimmying up and down the trunk, pecking for insects in the crevices of the bark. No sooner does it reach the top of the tree than it spirals back down like a mouse on steroids.

17 March

Today, I'm off to try some live hedge laying at Wells Farm in East Oxfordshire courtesy of the Berkshire, Buckinghamshire and Oxfordshire Wildlife Trust (BBOWT). Ever since Ron showed me how to lay a dead hedge using willow, I've been keen to learn more about our country traditions and the role they play in conserving nature.

Sadly, the UK has lost around a half of all its hedgerows since the 1950s, including many ancient hedgerows which are particularly precious to our wildlife. The shift in agricultural practices to more intensive farming is not the only reason; urban sprawl and the development of roads are also taking their toll, not to mention the depletion of hedges around villages and in private gardens like my own.

The impact continues to be devastating on our wildlife. Hedges are an invaluable habitat for vascular plants – 500 species of lignified plant grow in hedgerows – and they also provide nesting sites and food for birds as well as sustenance and shelter for moths, butterflies and other vital pollinators.

A healthy hedge is, as one of the bbowt instructors puts it, the avian equivalent of a Michelin-star restaurant, offering a rich spread of delicious insects, seeds and berries throughout the year. A healthy mixed hedgerow can offer blackberries and elderberries in late summer, rose hips, sloes and hawthorn in autumn and holly, rowan and ivy in winter. Of all the berries, though, ivy is the crown. According to the experts, just one gram of ivy berry has the same calorific value to our feathered friends as a whole bar of chocolate!

Wells Farm is a nature reserve and working farm which has moved away from intensive farming to more traditional methods of land management. It now boasts a beautiful hay meadow, two large amphibian-rich ponds, a bubbling brook and open fields of barley and wheat that have been edged with native wildflowers to draw in the spiders, beetles and other insects and act as natural pest controllers for the crops. The impact on biodiversity has been remarkable and the farm now attracts many rare farm birds including the yellowhammer, skylark and corn bunting.

Before mass migration to the cities in the nineteenth century, young men living in the country would have been taught by their fathers how to repair a stone wall, create a hazel hurdle or willow fence, coppice trees or lay a dead or live hedge, but with over eighty per cent of the UK population now living in towns and cities, it's no surprise that we have lost this connection with the countryside, and traditional rural crafts have gone out of fashion.

The overriding aim of live hedge laying is to regenerate growth, like coppicing a tree. The overgrown hedge is cut right back to its base and any tall stems are sliced down the middle so that one half of the stem or trunk can be bent over at an angle to form a neat, low hedge. The other half is left to regrow. It took our ten-man team of volunteers four hours to complete just a few metres of hedge, but the end result was neat and impressive and, most of all, I loved it! I felt a great sense of achievement at the end of the day and met a fantastic group of wildlife enthusiasts with an infectious energy and desire to preserve one of our enduring countryside traditions.

18 March

The evening sky has turned a deep burgundy and, across the valley, the sun is sinking slowly below the horizon like a fiery meteor. As the garden is shrouded in crepuscular grey, the trees between ourselves and our neighbour are thrown into silhouette, reminding me of a Thomas Sanchez painting. I feel privileged to be surrounded by so much beauty.

The days are getting longer and the evenings warmer and it will soon be possible to stay in the garden until well after 5 p.m., perhaps even without the encumbrance of a winter jacket. It feels mellow and peaceful as the shadows lengthen and I notice the mahonia "Charity", another of my new winter-flowering shrubs, has erupted into a profusion of exotic yellow flower. I'm delighted to see a large white-tailed bumblebee has already discovered its delicious nectar.

Every week, I'm discovering a new flower in the garden and not just in the borders. I walked past a clump of dog's mercury which had sprung up under the trees by our sheds, and found some Siberian squill, a pretty star-shaped bulbous perennial. Although I still like to dip into my father's *Observer's Book of Wildflowers*, I'm now using a free app on my mobile phone – *flora incognita* – which helps me identify any unknown species, like the squill, with a simple flash of my camera. It also keeps a record of my sightings and the date I saw them, which is handy.

19 March

A forceful Atlantic storm last night has left a field of debris in its wake. The front garden is strewn with leaves and branches and as I rush outside to check on the new trees, I run over an army of snails slithering across the terrace. The crunching sound is awful and I feel terrible looking at the gooey mess of crushed shells and body parts. In the past, I would have carelessly chucked the lot in the bin or over the fence but I try to salvage as many survivors as possible before leaving the mangled remains behind for the wildlife. Snails are rapacious consumers of garden plants but, like slugs, they play their part in the cycle of life and are a popular meal for hedgehogs, toads, frogs, slow-worms and some birds. With Georgie helping, I collect up the fallen sticks and branches and add them to my log piles around the garden perimeter.

According to a recent study by the Woodland Trust, UK woodland birds have declined by twenty-nine per cent since the 1970s. One reason for this is the loss of thicket and scrub on the woodland floor due to a reduction in traditional coppicing. When trees were cut to ground level every five years, the forest vegetation quickly regenerated itself and this sustained woodland birds, like the nightingale, that like to nest in thick undergrowth. Previous owners of our cottage may well have heard a nightingale in the garden, heralding in spring with its repertoire of sweet melodies, but hearing one now is as rare as hearing a cuckoo or turtle dove. Over ninety per cent have sadly disappeared from our countryside.

SPRING

And the Spring arose on the garden fair,
Like the spirit of love, felt everywhere;
And each flower and herb on earth's dark breast
Rose from the dreams of its wintry rest.
The snowdrop and then the violet,
Arose from the ground with warm rain wet;
And their breath was mixed with sweet odour sent
From the turf like the voice and instrument.
Percy Shelley

20 March

I'm sitting by the open French doors, listening to an orchestra of happy birdsong. It's the first official day of spring and the garden temperature is already into double figures. Georgie and Sooty are fully acclimatised to the unexpected heat and lying flat out on the terrace, lapping up the warm spring sunshine while a rotund cock pheasant and two robins peck at the ground just inches from their noses.

Georgie, more often than not, ignores the birds these days while at the venerable age of fifteen, Sooty has decided she's just too old for hunting. I found her slumped against the bird bath yesterday as a large pigeon bathed overhead.

25 March

I catch a glimpse of Ron's daughter, Julia, next door pushing his old wheelbarrow down to the vegetable patch just like he used to do. She's living permanently in his house now and carrying on his work in the garden. I still think of him, though, when I'm fishing out the algae from my pond, checking on my bird box or turning the compost. I think of my own father too every time I pass his willow or see a robin in the garden. Their memories and my wildlife garden are inextricably entwined.

I've finally started to identify the birds by their songs. It's not easy but there are many YouTube videos to help and the Royal Society for the Protection of Birds (RSPB) has produced its own bird song identifier. The dawn chorus is sometimes so sonorous and rich that I find it almost impossible to make head or tail of the different sounds, except for the robin, that is; its crystal-clear trill always stands out above the rest.

1 April

The prunus and cherry are competing for the prettiest blossom in the orchard and attracting plenty of attention from hungry bumblebees. It's a warm, mellow Sunday afternoon and I'm sitting outside, lapping up the sun and being lulled by the low, Gregorian chant of humming bees. With few cars on the road and only the occasional train rumbling in the valley, it's as if a microphone and speaker have been put in the back garden and the volume turned up to full capacity. A bumblebee symphony is playing, and I am the only audience.

2 April

I see my first bee-fly. It lands on the grass in front of me and starts poking its long, sharp proboscis into the soft centre of a pink primrose. It's joined by a sprightly black and white wagtail, which begins tail-pumping around the base of the bird feeder, and a newcomer to the garden – a hedge accentor.

Our swallows are back. They arrived last spring and they've returned again this year. I watch them congregate on the television aerial, their spiked tails bobbing up and down like feathered tongs. A juvenile with a less impressive tail streamer looks to be having a lesson on how to catch an airborne insect. It's amazing to think that these red-throated birds have migrated across two continents to reach my garden. They may choose to nest here every year if climate change or some associated natural disaster doesn't claim them first.

I still have days when I feel immense guilt and regret for not taking action sooner in my garden and I never completely lose the fear of what is happening to nature. I'm knocked sideways every time I hear yet another devastating report or survey about the impact of climate change and habitat loss on our native wildlife and I have to keep reminding myself that a better, more sustainable future, is still possible; nature can regenerate itself and biodiversity can be restored. My own garden is proof of that.

1 May

May Day and I've just seen a green woodpecker in the grass down by the meadow! It sensed my approach and soared away into the trees, but it was here, a flash of emerald-green and scarlet in the early sunshine. It's a sign the ants are back in the garden and, looking down, I notice a mass of fine, earthy mounds protruding through the grass. Passing one particularly prominent hillock, I catch a glimpse of coppery brown as a small vole or shrew disappears into a small round burrow beneath the billowy sward.

Having left the grass to grow over the winter, my wildflower lawn has become decidedly scruffy, but below the turf, peeping up from the long grass, I notice the first tender shoots of the yellow rattle I planted over three years ago. It's done what it was supposed to do – parasitise the grass – and has given vent to a variety of wildflowers, some I planted as plugs and seeds but most self-seeded. Among the spring growth is birds-foot trefoil, clover, wild primrose, wild daffodil, selfheal, daisy, buttercup and common dog violet. There are soft shades of colour everywhere and dainty flower buds on the cusp of blooming. A pretty fox-red bee joins me in the meadow, tempted out of hibernation by the balmy temperature and eager to find some energy-restoring nectar.

It's hard to believe that a few years ago this wild grassy patch was like a monochrome putting-green, cut so short you could see the earth underneath. I much prefer how it looks now – dappled, natural and bouncy, like a bouffant hairdo. There's energy in the grass, a voluptuousness which heralds new life and, each year, I'm impatient to see what new surprises it will throw forth.

I'm like a child again, in the thrall of nature. It's not just the meadow that has burst into life. The borders, left to naturalise with the wild, are a profusion of light blue forget-me-not, pink and white primrose and yellow cowslip. It's as if Persephone, the Greek goddess of springtime, has left her indelible mark in every corner of the garden. A small field of yellow buttercups has sprung up under the apple trees, and a patch of sweet violet by the meadow.

5 May

The pond is still in its infancy, but I'm noticing more and more bugs coursing through the water, and today there are pond skaters sliding over the surface. They skate from one marginal plant to another, searching for tiny insects under the surface of the water. It will be interesting to see if they lay their eggs in the pond and multiply over the summer; if so, the birds will be pleased. They make a tasty snack for our feathered friends. The rushes and marginals I planted by the side of the pond are sprouting up above the surface and there's less algae than I feared thanks to the deep oxygenating plants at the bottom and my new solar-powered fountain, which is circulating the water successfully.

10 May

This morning, the trees are full of multicoloured sparkles in the early sunshine and the leaf buds of the alder and beech are beginning to unfurl with the promise of a warm day ahead. Pretty clusters of white flowers are out for the first time on the mountain ash I planted in memory of Ron, and I think of him whenever I pass. He loved watching the different birds visiting the tall rowan by our gate and would often collect up the fallen berries to make jam.

15 May

A gang of willow tits has descended on the bird feeders. There must be at least six in total and they are joined by two or three long-tailed tits eager to share the feeding frenzy. This is the second time I've seen flocks of the same species of bird in the garden and I'm hoping the females are on the hunt for suitable nesting sites in our rotten tree trunks. Just to glimpse a willow tit is a privilege these days. When the babies hatch in late spring, they will need a constant supply of aphids, caterpillars, flies and spiders to survive – one of many reasons why I've stopped using pesticides in the garden. Like many of our native birds, willow tits are in drastic decline and we need to do everything in our power to protect them.

A bird which isn't yet threatened but frequents our new garden, is the red-and-black-feathered greater spotted woodpecker, and I often see adults visiting our nut feeder early in the morning or hear the reverberating drill of one rapping against a hollow tree trunk *–Magic.*

20 May

A solitary pied wagtail is watching the swallows from its high perch on our roof. After a few minutes, another wagtail flies in and there's a frantic tail-pump before they fly off together in the direction of the trees. Dusk falls and a pair of wood pigeons take up their roosting position, one above the other on the silver birch, the mossy branches acting as their passerine bunkbed. These two pigeons have returned to the exact same night spot for the last few days, snuggling down together as the shadows lengthen. In time, their silhouettes disappear, absorbed completely by the darkness.

They may not be top of my must-have-in-the-garden list, but the wood pigeon is thousands of years old and their remarkable homing instinct and affinity with humans has made them useful messengers, particularly in wartime, often risking their lives in the process. They may be common and cumbersome, even reviled at times, but I'm happy to have them roosting in my garden.

1 June

The more I do in my wildlife garden, the more I find I want to do, and today I'm planting up a new wildlife border at the front of the house. To achieve all-year colour, I've chosen a mix of ornamental cherry blossom which blooms in early spring, purple salvia, verbena and English lavender for summer and a gorgeous rose-flowered buddleia and orange rudbeckia to keep the nectar flowing well into autumn. For winter colour and scent, I'm planting snowdrops and aconites and two large white-scented sarcococca that are a magnet, I'm told, for night moths.

I'm also taking a leaf out of my father's book and sprinkling wildflower seed in all the empty spaces, including along the edge of the drive. Instead of grass, the sides will now be a mass of dropwort, cats-ear, lady's bedstraw, St John's wort, bellflower and poppy.

My mother is here to help me and has donated a scented clematis to the border which she remembers trailing up the side of our old coach house. We find a good shady spot for it up against the front wall, and she sings a merry tune as I dig a deep hole while bees and flies buzz around her large floral hat.

'Your father always said the clematis I planted was one of the best climbers in the garden for wildlife,' my mother said wistfully, as I smooth the earth around the plant stem with my foot.

'The flowers attracted all kinds of bees, moths and butterflies and the birds used the bushy foliage to nest in. We planted several in the end and I remember your father swooning every time he got a whiff of gorgeous scent; it used to send him into a strange reverie.'

Last autumn, I noticed for the first time the overgrown shrubs and beech hedge on our southern boundary were shrouded in wild clematis or "old man's beard", as it is more widely known. On closer inspection, I uncovered a charm of goldfinches nestled in the tangled branches and watched, intrigued, as they tucked into the seeds of the white candyfloss flowers.

Our final job of the day is to plant two "Paul's Scarlet" hawthorn trees at the edge of the new borders by the front door. I'm hoping they will produce thorny stems and clusters of crimson blossoms in spring which the bees and other pollinators will love.

5 June

Magenta, white and lilac crocuses have sprung up all over the borders like splashes of vivid colour on a Monet painting while the orchard has become a yellow meadow of wild primroses and narcissi. I've seen bumblebees of all colour, shape and size flying in to savour the early nectar, including a newcomer to the garden today – a tawny bee. I delve back into my father's nature books and discover that tawny bees will burrow under stones or grass to build a home, which might account for the volcano-shaped mounds of soil that have appeared by one of the log piles.

Sitting on the front terrace admiring Ron's copper beech which has burst into a glossy, red effervescence, I look up and see a number of small bumblebees swarming by the side of one of our eaves. On closer inspection, I see they're white-tailed bumblebees and they've made their home inside the cracked mortar. The large queen swoops down as if to check me out as I drink my coffee just a few feet from her hive and then returns, reassured, to her male contingent of would-be lovers buzzing around the hole.

17 June

I'm consciously trying to not disturb any nesting birds as I work in the borders or under the trees. The robin and garden warbler are two species that like to nest in low, dense shrubbery, and I remember inadvertently unearthing a warbler's nest last summer and watching with horror as the tiny fledglings scuttled off, terrified, to find shelter. I don't expect they survived after that.

Half a dozen blue tits are feeding in the back garden, and I've seen a couple building a compact mossy nest in a high branch of the old rambling rose on our west-facing wall. They've been swooping down past an upstairs window with sprigs of grass and twigs in their beaks, occasionally hitting the glass with a loud, alarming thud. I've also seen two new nests high up in the field maple, one in a small sycamore and one in the acer griseum on the front lawn and imagine they belong to songbirds too.

Seeing the nests reminds me to check on Ron's bird box, the first bird home we installed together. To my joy, I find it is occupied; there's a loose strand of straw hanging over the box edge and when I creep closer, I can hear a faint chirruping inside. Fledglings in my bird box! I wait in expectation to see if they are robins or long-tailed tits.

20 June

The rain overnight has released the sweet-scented aromas of hyacinth, osmanthus and skimmia in the garden and the woodland is infused with a potent allure of wild garlic. I lean down and pick a garlic leaf, eager to infuse its legendary aroma. Back in pre-medieval times, when our countryside was wild, forested and populated by large predators, brown bears would emerge in spring to the pungent draw of wild garlic and they would root up the soil to feast on the bulbs. The clue to this seasonal ursine ritual is in the plant's Latin name – allium ursinum – which translates as "bear's leek." Although my newly-rewilded wood is way off attracting back brown bears or even wild boar, for that matter, I do notice a mass of hungry bumblebees and hover flies swarming the garlic's white star-burst flowers.

Elsewhere on the woodland floor, I spot pink and lilac primrose, Siberian bugloss and white anemone, and then some unusual pink and white bluebells among the more traditional varieties. I assume they have always been here; I just haven't noticed them before. The explosion of scent and colour is attracting a rich diversity of pollinating insects and the long grass (now uncut since September) is emitting a continual contented hum. I see my second new butterfly of the year; it's a small speckled wood, a handsome butterfly with a distinctive wing hem of tiger-eye dots. I watch as it flutters past and lands on the wooden fence by the drive. All this gentle activity adds to a sense that spring is on the wane and summer's warmth is tempting out the first of the garden's winged creatures. The season is changing before my very eyes.

SUMMER

I love to see the summer beaming forth
And white wool sack clouds sailing to the north
I love to see the wildflowers come again
And mare blobs stain with gold the meadow drain
And water lilies whiten on the floods
Where reed clumps rustle like a wind shook wood
Where from her hiding place the Moor hen pushes
and seeks her flag nest floating in bull rushes
I like the willow leaning half way o'er
The clear deep lake to stand upon its shore
I love the hay grass when the flowerhead swings
To summer winds and insects happy wings
That sport about the meadow the bright day
And see bright beetles in the clear lake play
John Clare

21 June

June solstice – the astronomical start of summer
– and our new wildflower meadow has been
transformed into a bright yellow field of miniature
sun orbs. Clusters of dandelions have sprouted
everywhere, reminding me of my father's garden and
playing the dandelion "clock" game with friends when
I was a young girl. Dad's uncut lawn would always be a mass of
dandelions and daisies in June and July, providing me with hours of
innocent fun and, by the end of the summer, the mirror in my bedroom
would be festooned with wilted flower chains and my flower press full of
faded blooms. Our childhood games were simple in the 1970s – there was
no internet and no mobile phones – yet I never remember getting bored
in the garden. As long as I had nature's gifts to play with, I was forever

happy and absorbed. I highly doubt that making a daisy or dandelion chain is top of a child's "to do" list these days.

I take a seat under my father's willow by the meadow and my heart leaps when I hear the sibilant chirping of crickets in the grass. It's the first time, and what a heavenly sound it is, so unexpected and welcome. Crickets and grasshoppers have suffered a drastic decline in distribution over the last fifty years, so much so that the leggy creatures are now officially endangered. Hearing their sonorous stridulations today – such a familiar sound of my childhood – has brought a smile to my face.

I focus my binoculars on the long grass. A sleepy bumblebee is the first to visit, landing on one of the largest dandelions and wobbling on the nectar-filled surface like a tipsy reveller. The bumblebee is quickly followed by a nifty honeybee that flits from one flower to another, as if uncertain where to land. Then, out of the corner of my eye, I spot a large, dark-brown butterfly enjoying the warm sunshine amid the fresh dandelion leaves. It looks, from a distance, like a miniature manta ray submerged in a sea of green but, as I creep closer, I can see it's a beautiful peacock butterfly, its wings fully outstretched as if infusing the sun's energy. The peacock was one of my favourite butterflies as a child. I used to stare in awe at the four vivid eyelets on its forewings – so like peacock eyes it was uncanny – and was convinced they were winking at me every time the butterfly flexed its wings. I stand and stare again as this newly-emerged giant sucks up the revitalising warmth. Soon, it will need to feed and find a mate but, for now, it remains tranquil and sun-soaked.

Delving into my father's wildflower manuals later, I re-read the salient facts about the simple, much-maligned dandelion and how important this flower is in our ecosystem. Its nectar doesn't just attract butterflies; it is a vital food source for moths, bees, beetles and hoverflies as well, while the dandelion seeds are popular with insects and birds, particularly the goldfinch.

Each day, I enjoy recording in my new diary the different species of flora and fauna I uncover in my burgeoning wildlife garden, and each day,

I learn a little bit more about their importance in our precious ecosystem. It's as if I'm peeling back, layer by layer, the knowledge my father installed in me over forty years ago, bringing it back to the surface, to the forefront of my psyche, never to be lost again, I hope. And the knowledge seems to have even greater resonance now than it did when I was a child; it feels more pertinent, more visceral somehow and more vital.

Currently, the UK has sixty-six wild mammal species, 574 bird species, six reptile, seven amphibian and 27,000 insect species (including 2,500 different moth varieties and fifty-nine species of butterfly). It will take me years to even scrape the surface of the knowledge I need to protect even a tiny proportion of these precious creatures, but it's a quest worth pursuing if I want to help stem the increasing decline in biodiversity.

There is, of course, no guarantee of success, however miraculous nature is. So much depends on collective action and changing preconceived prejudices. I've seen first-hand how important the simple dandelion is to our native wildlife and how common nettle, ivy and bramble have vital roles to play in our ecosystem but how easy will it be to change other people's attitudes to these unpopular species, enough to preserve the wonderful creatures that rely on them? I've learnt that the jay, a bird most associated with stealing other birds' eggs, is, in fact, a crucial link in the survival of our precious oak and, according to scientists, jays have been sustaining our national tree since the last ice-age through the simple distribution of acorns. When I see a jay now in the garden, I resist the urge to shoo it away just as I resist the urge to mow the grass or dispose of dead wood and cuttings. It's all about knowledge at the end of the day – knowledge, commitment and a bit of luck!

1 July

After nearly five years creating a wildlife haven and studying the flora and fauna which inhabit it, my family and friends are beginning to lean on me more and more for advice. But there are downsides to this, as Ed is discovering. He feels the increasing need to ask my permission before he does anything in the garden, in case he inadvertently destroys an important wildlife habitat or upsets one of my wilding projects, and my response is often unnecessarily curt.

'Can I mow the orchard?'

'I would rather you didn't!'

'Why?'

'Because I'm letting the wildflowers grow.'

'Can I take those planks of decaying wood to the dump?'

'No need.'

'Why?'

'Because I can use them for insect shelters.'

'Can we get rid of the foxes in the garden? Georgie keeps rolling in the poo.'

'Not sure that would be a good idea; they keep the grey squirrel numbers down and the greys disturb the birds, strip the bark off the trees and eat apple and pear buds.'

And so on. While knowledge may well be power in my case, my mother has noticed that my new-found enthusiasm for nature does take over at times and, in true spirit, she's the first to comment:

'Ed's looking a bit drawn these days. Is he happy, darling, with the amount of time you're spending in the garden? Have you tried involving him a bit more? Let him take control of a few things? It's his garden too.'

She's right, of course. I need to make much more effort to involve Ed and take him with me on my quest; he mustn't be made to feel like one of Georgie's trapped pheasants.

10 July

I wake to another fine, warm day. It hasn't rained for a week, and I'm concerned about the new trees drying out. I've managed to create a hose long enough to reach 150 metres or so to the furthest sapling at the bottom of the garden.

It takes me two hours to water all the trees, but I find the process therapeutic and peaceful. I enjoy just looking and feeling, smelling and listening, and it's a chance for me to take in every little detail of nature: the tiny buds forming on the new trees, a spider weaving its way through the long dewy grass, a curled ivy leaf containing a tiny caterpillar or a pretty butterfly flitting from one flower to another. I notice the changing hues and light displays in the wood and, if I time it right, I might see our stoat scurrying along the back of the hedge.

15 July

I heard an owl this morning before dawn, a staccato pipe-sound resembling the whooping of a male marking his territory. Could it be we have a breeding pair of little owls in the garden for the first time? I can hardly contain my excitement and rush outside to check for any likely nesting spots in the garden. There are plenty – rotting trunks, decaying log piles and my nest boxes.

Streaks of sunlight are piercing the woodland canopy and catching the iridescent wingtips of thousands of tiny insects taking their first flights. The grass is sparkling with early dew, and the fresh growth and honey blossom from the weeping pear are breathing fresh aromas into the air.

The new trees have burst forth with leaves, miniature replicas of their mature neighbours. In an open glade, I discover two self-seeded horse chestnut saplings sprouting from the long grass like emerald palms. Unless I'm mistaken, these are the first conker trees to germinate in the garden – great news for the woodland wildlife. The pink and white flowers will be a mass of bees and other pollinating insects in summer, and the pointed leaves are a valuable food source for caterpillars, including the leaf-miner moth that blue tits feed on.

Later, standing on the terrace with a cup of tea, I look out for the little mouse I saw scampering about in the geranium, but he's nowhere to be seen. Perhaps he's resting safely in the neat round hole I saw yesterday by the shed. As evening starts to cloak the garden in dark shadows, I take a stroll down to the wildflower meadow. Sitting quietly by the pond, a squadron of pipistrelle bats perform an aerial loop-the-loop display in front of me, swooping down to drink from the new solar fountain before disappearing back into the canopy of darkness.

20 July

A perfect mid-summer morn. Not a cloud in the sky, and I'm surrounded by gentle humming as I plant teasel and cornflower plugs in my wildflower meadow. The honey and bumblebees are out in force today including an unusual bee with an auburn tail. It's exceptionally pretty and not one I've seen before. I carefully reach for my father's field glasses and watch as it feasts on a willow catkin, its furry abdomen almost entirely covered in yellow pollen.

As I move the binoculars a little to the left, I notice a white-tailed bumblebee enjoying the green alkanet. It has found an ingenious way of abseiling down the blue forget-me-not flowers and is taking small sips from each one. The green alkanet is spreading fast under the beech like a blue hem on an emerald curtain. Zooming in on the leaves, I'm intrigued to see they are covered with yellow and black scarlet tiger caterpillars. These striking larvae will pupate into even more glorious white, red and yellow-spotted moths later in the summer – a treat worth waiting for.

The adage that our lawns are dormant meadows just waiting to grow couldn't be truer in my newly formed wildlife garden. Every week, I'm treated to a new wildflower emerging in the meadow. Oxeye daisy, buttercup, herb Robert, birds-foot trefoil, white stitchwort and clover have all raised their heads above the grass, but my biggest prize to date has been the discovery of three stunning new orchids – the pyramidal orchid, common spotted orchid and the bee orchid. All have naturalised in my meadow and are spreading.

The yellow rattle I planted is doing an effective job in keeping the grass down and allowing the plug plants and seeds to grow. My meadow will be complete when the blue cornflowers, golden marigolds and crimson poppies hopefully appear in July.

25 July

A morning shower has soaked the thirsty borders and hedges and released some powerful scents. I'm pleased to see there is still plenty of late-summer colour in the flowerbeds and the pollinators are out in force enjoying the nectar. Since leaving the borders to naturalise with the wildflowers and weeding less, I've had an influx of tall yellow verbascum and evening primrose; where they've come from is anyone's guess but they complement the echinacea and anemone well and bring fresh colour and shape to the borders. A meadow brown butterfly flits past and lands on one of the blooms, burrowing itself into the welcoming spread of petals. After satisfying itself with nectar, it moves on to a luscious white bramble blossom for an aperitif. I notice the furry leaves of the verbascum are being slowly shredded by a contingent of large white butterfly caterpillars.

By afternoon, the warm sun has soaked up the residual raindrops on the flowers and spread itself over the meadow like an orange fire glow. I can see tiny flying insects reflected off the surface of the pond and watch as a pair of azure blue damselflies swoop down to investigate.

I'm admiring the display when a bright green brimstone butterfly lands on the purple lilac and fans itself in the afternoon heat. The sun has drawn out clouds of insects and pollinators, and in the course of just half an hour, I see twelve different varieties of butterfly descend on the wildflowers, including my first holly blue, an admiral, six large whites, a meadow brown and an orange-tipped butterfly. I could be witnessing a lepidoptera summer picnic.

1 August

I've taken to sitting by the meadow most afternoons with my field glasses focused on the pond and long grass. Today I'm watching a kestrel as it gyrates on the warm thermals above, its keen eye fixed on the ground and its long sharp claws ready to pounce on any unsuspecting vole or grasshopper.

5 August

The woodland glade is maintaining its colour and I've been busy recording the wildflowers as they bloom on my *flora incognita* app. The app's observation history reads like a woodland wildflower anthology – selfheal, hogweed, cow parsley, wood crane's-bill, sweet violet, campion and field scabious. I've also seen a solitary pink and white common spotted orchid nestled in the long grass. This is my first sighting of an orchid in the woodland glade and, as I kneel down in the grass to take a closer look, a pretty black-spotted fritillary butterfly floats by on the soft summer breeze.

10 August

The house martins are back and have taken up residence in the cupped nest under the garage roof used earlier in the summer by the swallows. They stare down at me with somnolent eyes every time I go to my car, perched on a high beam like an audience looking down from the "gods" in a theatre.

20 August

I think about my father more than ever. Barely a day goes by without his ghost creeping into my thoughts or me regretting something I should have said to him before he died. I miss him most when I am in the garden, potting or scattering wildflower seeds or checking my insect hotel, and he's there with me whenever I'm experiencing the joy of finding a new species or listening to a robin sing.

I heard the exquisite sound of a cuckoo for the first time this morning and I could sense my father by my side whispering to me to be silent and listen.

Often the new discoveries bring back amusing memories which have lain dormant for years. I woke recently to find the lawn pock-marked with brown earthy piles, the first tell-tale signs of a visiting mole. I immediately thought of Dad and smiled. I always believed moles were rather cute as a child, but my father tried everything in his power to deter them from the garden, despite their ability to regenerate the soil.

He started off planting daffodils and euphorbia close to the lawn edge, believing their toxic bulbs would discourage the moles. When this failed, he tried sticking moth balls and a mixture of coffee granules and castor oil down the tunnels, but this failed too. Almost at his wits' end, he's discovered a new invention – a battery-powered mole scarer – which he eagerly bought at vast expense and placed against the molehills, making our lawn look a bit like a mini-golf course. Unfortunately, the scarers were useless and emitted such a high pitch alarm that their only legacy was to keep my mother awake at night.

In the end, Dad simply had to accept defeat, as he did with the rabbits, and leave the moles to the mercy of nature.

1 September

I'm standing, transfixed, at the bedroom window, clutching my father's field glasses. A family of three green woodpeckers are picnicking in the back garden, their shiny red crowns radiant in the early morning sunlight. Every so often, one of the adults hops across to the mottled juvenile and deposits a grub or ant into its long open beak. There ensues a lesson in how to forage successfully before a sudden disturbance in the bushes distracts the happy family gathering and they soar off into the thick canopy of the fruit trees.

AUTUMN

Season of mists and mellow fruitfulness,
Close bosom-friend of the maturing sun;
Conspiring with him how to load and bless
With fruit the vines that round the thatch-eves run;
To bend with apples the moss'd cottage-trees,
And fill all fruit with ripeness to the core;
To swell the gourd, and plump the hazel shells
With a sweet kernel; to set budding more,
And still more, later flowers for the bees,
Until they think warm days will never cease,
For summer has o'er-brimm'd their clammy cells.
John Keats

21 September

My new woodland has become an arboretum, at last, with the full range
of equinox colour: russet, ochre, copper, crimson, yellow, orange and
brown. Only the oak leaves are still clinging on to their summer green. I
feel a real sense of pride strolling through the trees today and staring up
at the array of dazzling colours. Four years ago, this stretch of land was
nothing more than barren grass with only a sprinkling of the original
woodland left. It now looks like a genuine wood and, with the exception
of one larch, the trees have more than doubled in height and width,
proving that nature can be restored quickly, with a little tender loving
care. I particularly love the woody aroma that the trees emit after it has
rained. If I stand still and breath deeply, I can feel my whole body relax
and warm childhood memories stir deep within my psyche.

1 October

The woodland floor is green
and lush and covered in

fungi. Different sized mushrooms and toadstools in all colours of the rainbow have sprung up like parasols in the long grass, along the bark of decaying logs and up against the dead trunks of the trees. There are brown and white mushroom caps, orange jelly-ear mushrooms and the iconic scarlet and white fly agaric, which I remember from my fairy tales.

The most prolific fungus though is a dirt-brown, pear-shaped puffball, which looks like acne and explodes when knocked, spraying mucky-coloured spores of dry dust all over the damp grass.

The flush of fungi is good news for the trees. The mushroom, or toadstool, I see above the ground is the spore-bearing fruit. The main body of the fungus lives underground and, according to my mushroom guide, forms a long dense network of threads (the mycelium) that can stretch for miles, attaching themselves to tree roots, grasses and other plants. This "woodwide web" as it's aptly called is a lifeline for wildlife, providing plants with vital nutrients from the soil and absorbing carbohydrates back down from the plants into the earth. It is also used by trees to communicate with other trees. If one tree is being threatened by a disease, insects or a harmful fungus, it can send a warning signal via the underground threads to others close by.

I shudder to think how busy this subterranean network must have been during my two-decade reign of terror in the garden before the wonders of wildlife gardening taught me otherwise.

5 October

The late-summer colour has all but faded from the garden and there are just a few hardy wildflowers left. Among the hangers-on are devil's bit scabious and red campion. Their single blooms are attracting a disproportionate amount of interest from hungry insects eager to nab the last of the nectar before winter finally closes off their supplies.

Seeing the campion always reminds me of Ron and our afternoon erecting the bird box. He would be delighted with how the garden looks now and rightly proud of the fruits of his gigantean efforts. He will always be a part of this garden, and I have no doubt his soul lives on in his daughter, Julia. She seems as committed as he was to preserving nature.

15 October

We have Ron's favourite bird – a song thrush – in the garden guarding the white berries on the mountain ash. It stays till dusk, marking its territory, and hopping from branch to branch. Only the feisty robin dares confront it. Perched on one of the highest claw-shaped branches, surrounded by a sea of white, the thrush bursts into song, a rich and flute-like lament that pierces the eerie silence of the morning. I feel privileged to witness the unexpected, virtuoso performance.

20 October

The days are drawing in, and the October sun is quickly losing its power but, despite the shift in temperature, there is still plenty of insect, bird and animal activity around the pond. A warty toad has taken up residence under a clump of wild geranium by the side of the water, and, if I'm down in the meadow in late afternoon, I can still sometimes glimpse a field vole emerging from its burrow under a tufted clump of grass, or a weasel slinking through the hole in our fence on its way back home.

25 October

A late burst of "Indian" summer and the butterflies are flocking to the pink and purple buddleias for one last feeding frenzy. My new salvias are also attracting attention from pollinators. I saw a hummingbird hawkmoth hovering like a kestrel above one this afternoon before zoning in on a glossy red bloom and stabbing its long thin proboscis into its soft centre. Later, I caught another large peacock butterfly sunning itself against a warm brick on our terrace and a copper skittering past to feed on the alstroemerias. There is no lack of insect activity in our garden despite it being late in the year and this proves to me, more than anything, that my project is working, that wilding can restore biodiversity.

There's never a dull moment in my wildlife garden. Autumn, always my favourite month, tosses and turns like the waters of the Thames, bringing new species, colours and scents to the garden before winter's wave rolls in and sweeps everything away.

NINETEEN
BLACKBERRY FOOL

Trailing a large wicker basket and long walking stick, Simon was reluctantly following me up the footpath to the field. He didn't like picking blackberries and would rather have been lying on his bunk bed reading his latest *Biggles* book.

I was much keener. It was a chance to go back to the field where I saw the poppies with Dad last summer and find new butterflies. It was also my one opportunity to eat as many big, juicy berries as I could without my mother telling me off. By the time she saw me with a large black rim around my mouth and bits of pith in my teeth, she was too distracted to care.

My mother was striding up ahead, oblivious to my brother's foul

mood and intent on one thing and one thing only: reaching the blackberry bushes before our neighbours did. She was dressed in a pair of pink flared trousers, a floral shirt with a diamond-shaped collar, and a wide-brimmed hat festooned with a long rose-printed scarf.

At all stretches of the imagination, it was a totally inappropriate outfit for the occasion but one which she insisted on wearing despite my father's inauspicious prediction that she would be stung to death by bees (presumably thinking she was a large flower).

'You are ridiculous, Timmy,' she said, as we exited the garden via the small back gate, 'this is Kent, not the Amazon Rainforest.'

I was still imagining her covered in black hungry bees when I heard her calling from the field. 'Do hurry up, children! I can see some corkers here, and we don't want the Blakemores getting to them first. Your father would never forgive me.'

Blackberries always had this weird effect on my mother. She got strangely territorial about them, so much so that my brother and I reckoned she would rather have fought to the death than give up her blackberry picking zone. For years, we thought the curved walking sticks were for that very purpose.

When we caught up with her in the field, we could see the bushes were groaning with large juicy berries. My mother directed us, like an army officer, to begin our hunt at the opposite end of the field to her, so, as she put it, we could 'maximise our chances of filling our baskets with the best of the crop before the dreaded neighbours arrive'.

I was fine with the command. It gave me ample opportunity to consume as many berries as I could, without my mother's interference, before we had to return home. My brother was less enthused; it meant further for him to walk.

After identifying a particularly promising bush, I dutifully knelt on the hard, prickly ground so Simon could stand on my back and reach for the high branches. As I winced with every prick of bramble, I held my breath and could feel Simon rising up on tiptoe. He must have stretched just that little bit too far because one of his feet suddenly slipped and, before I could grab his other ankle, he had crashed down into the bramble bush, his punnet spewing out the few berries he had just picked. He let out a loud scream, and my mother raced over. She helped him up and I could see he was oozing blackberry and blood from several cuts on his leg. His face was also streaming with black-liquid tears. Mum lent him a hanky to wipe up the blood, then kissed his cheek and with characteristic heartiness, said:

'Chin up, there's a good chap. All the best blackberry pickers get pricked. Try that bush over there. We all need a full basket before we go home.'

I watched, feigning sympathy, as poor defeated Simon hobbled off in the direction of his next challenge, and then turned quickly to a particularly promising bush I had spotted earlier. I wasn't going to miss my best chance of a bramble feast.

Making our way back down the footpath, our punnets laden with the stolen fruit, we must have looked like war-wounded soldiers returning from the Somme. Our shirts were torn and stained black, our hair was matted with prickly stems, and every bit of our exposed body parts were scarred red with cuts. But my mother beamed from ear to ear. She knew her troops had scored a major victory over the Blakemores, and Dad would be delighted with the rich spoils. He would have enough berries now to last until the spring and this would satisfy his perpetual longing for blackberry fool and crumble.

13 November

Today, on the eighth anniversary of my father's death, I'm going blackberry picking again with my mother, for old times' sake. It's been forty years since we last shared this particular family tradition, and I'm not sure who is more excited – my mother or me.

It's a misty, dank morning and Mum is togged out in her pink designer jacket and colourful wide-brimmed hat, not dissimilar to the one I remember her wearing when we picked blackberries back in the 1970s.

'It's the only one I could find,' she says, smiling.

'I think it's gorgeous,' I reply a little enviously.

I lend her a large punnet, and we weave our way across the grass and past the pond which is now shrouded in wheat-length grass and faded flowers.

I glance quickly at the hole in the fence and the clump of garden debris where I photographed the stoat earlier in the year. I can see the wire around the hole has been pushed back and more passageways have been excavated into the mound. I'm intrigued to know what other animal might be living there; I'm hoping a hedgehog or fox.

'Looks like you've got a rabbit warren,' my mother says provocatively.

'I like to think of it as a gateway to freedom,' I say whimsically. 'A bona fide green corridor linking our garden to the wider countryside.'

'Well, just as long as it's not a rabbit run, darling. Your father would certainly not approve!'

'I think he would now,' I whisper under my breath.

We continue through the gate and into the cemetery where I know the hedges still have a few sloes and blackberries left. My mother's hawk eye manages to spot some juicy ones. She's not lost her knack of spotting a "corker", but being less mobile these days, she stands at a distance and observes, as I clamber into the bush.

I use her walking stick to hack my way through the prickly foliage and a robin joins me, alighting on a nearby branch. With its big black eyes and pulsating breast feathers bristling in the breeze, it could be the same robin I saw on the oak, several years ago now, the one which helped inspire me to start of my wilding project, and my mind skips back to that time. I was dominated then by confusion and fear and guilt, but I'm not anymore. I'm much more positive these days, partly because I feel I am doing something, finally, to help our natural world. I have a purpose once again in my life, and I have glorious memories of how our countryside once looked and how it could look, again, in the future. I couldn't be happier.

I'm distracted by a large red admiral which has sunk its tongue into a large berry and it reminds me of the white admiral I saw on the honeysuckle when I was still my father's little follower. I'm minded to leave the remaining fruits for the over-wintering insects, mammals and birds to enjoy, but with my mother looking over my shoulder, I have to be surreptitious.

Our baskets are only half full as we pass through the turnstile and take the footpath down to the wood, scouring the line of ancient hazel and hawthorn for berries along the way. We skirt the wood, rise up through the meadow where the summer flowers are brown and drooped and continue our bramble ramble along the top of the hill. The hedges there are tall and, to my mother's delight, still teeming with fruit.

'At last, some real corkers,' she says with verve, and I watch, amused, as she plunges her stick into the entangled mass of bramble and pulls down a massive branch. 'Quickly, pick them before I let go!' she hollers, as if her life depends on it.

It's getting late by the time we finish, and a grey mist has descended on the hillside. Looking down the valley, I see that the village is shrouded in fog; only the uppermost tip of the sandstone belltower of St Thomas's Church is peeping through the haze. It's as if civilisation has silently disappeared. The air smells dank, and the only sound to break the silence is the sudden piercing squeal of a red kite.

I turn and walk back along the footpath with my mother. I'm glad I've had this afternoon with her; she's not getting any younger, and it's lovely to revisit something we shared when I was a child.

'Haven't we done well?' she says, with a beaming smile as she shakes her blackberries enthusiastically. She looks rosy-cheeked and invigorated with all the fresh air, and her wide-brimmed hat has kept her hair immaculate despite the pervading damp. 'I think we probably have enough berries for two crumbles and a fool. Would you like me to cook them up for you and Ed when we get home? For old times' sake.'

'That would be wonderful, if you could,' I reply warmly. 'You always did the best blackberry fool.'

There's a parcel waiting for me on the doorstep when we get back to the house. I put it on the stairs thinking it must be a late birthday present and go through to the kitchen to put the kettle on and make my mother some hot-buttered crumpets.

We sit at the table chatting and sipping tea while she removes the prickly stems from the berries along with a retinue of tiny spiders and flies. We chat about my childhood, the garden and, of course, Dad, and she tells me about her spontaneous decision to scatter his ashes over the garden before she left the family home.

'It was where he would have wanted to go, in his beloved garden, beside his roses and wildflowers. Almost the last thing he said to me before he died was 'Claire, whatever you do, don't leave me like an ancient relic on your mantel piece. I want to be put back into the earth to feed the plants.'

And then with a smile and a wink, she adds, 'Of course, I was wearing my best bikini and hat for the job.'

After tea, I leave her in the kitchen with her blackberries and go next door to sit by the fire and open my parcel. It's in a heavily bound envelope and when I do finally manage to prize it open, it's not a present as I expected but a small book that falls out onto my lap. On the cover is a drawing of a pretty, dappled deer, and inside is a scruffy piece of paper.

My heart misses a beat. I recognise my long lost childhood diary immediately and I cry out in surprise.

'Mum!' I shout, adrenalin cruising through my veins, 'it's my nature diary and a note from Simon. He says he found it tucked away in his old chest of books from the coach house. It's here with a poem from Dad.'

I'm holding the journal to my chest when she rushes in.

'I can't believe it, after all these years,' she says with tears welling in her eyes. 'That's your father for you, in a nutshell. Never could throw anything away. He's come up trumps this time.'

She gives me a warm hug and then leaves me, quietly, to my memories. I lean back in my chair and open the journal, tentatively at first. My hands are shaking and my heart feels as if it might explode out of my chest. There's a child's drawing of a young tawny fox on the opening page, followed by a short, handwritten story in blue ink entitled *Ginger the Fox*. The entry is dated 1 January 1978.

The young fox in our garage is called Ginger and she has travelled all the way from Tunbridge Wells, a big town where life is dangerous and dreary for a fox. She has been forced to leave the town to find food and somewhere cosy and warm for the winter. Our garage is full of hay and it feels safe. Ginger hopes she can stay there forever and raise her young, without the fear of evil hunters. She quickly hides in the hay feeling comfort for the first time in her life and although she is ravenous, she falls fast asleep in her blissful hideaway. During the night, it snows but Ginger remains warm in the soft hay and sleeps like a log. In the morning she wakes up to find the ground is covered in a soft, white carpet. She's about to venture out of her den when she smells a strong scent which reminds her of town. It's the scent of humans and out of the corner of her black eye, she sees four brown eyes staring back at her from the entrance to the garage. They belong to a man in a thick overcoat and a young girl in a woollen hat. She's afraid at first but the humans are smiling at her and look kind and she knows immediately that they are her friends. At last, she thinks, I have reached my dreamland. I don't need to run anymore. I can raise my cubs here.

I then read the poem which my father has left me – a handwritten reminder of our very special childhood bond and a garden I will now never forget.

LEISURE

WHAT is this life if, full of care,
We have no time to stand and stare?
No time to stand beneath the boughs,
And stare as long as sheep and cows:
No time to see, when woods we pass,
Where squirrels hide their nuts in grass:
No time to see, in broad daylight,
Streams full of stars, like skies at night:
No time to turn at Beauty's glance,
And watch her feet, how they can dance:
No time to wait till her mouth can
Enrich that smile her eyes began?
A poor life this is if, full of care,
We have no time to stand and stare
W H Davies

Love Dad xxx

A WORD FROM
THE AUTHOR

After spending four glorious years returning my cottage garden to nature, I'm now a full convert to wilding and its multitudinous benefits. Not only has wilding restored my garden to its former glory, rich in biodiversity, scent, sound and colour, it has also brought tremendous peace and happiness to me and my family. I hope my green odyssey, charted in this book, can inspire other gardeners to take up arms in defence of our wildlife. However big or small our private outdoor space, we can all make a difference to biodiversity and, ultimately, to our planet.

There is no doubt that our natural world is facing an existential crisis. In just fifty years, over half our native flora and fauna has sharply declined, and creatures and plants which I took for granted as a child, like the cornflower, the nightingale, the skylark, the grasshopper, the turtle dove, the hare, the barn owl, the centipede, the song thrush and the hedgehog are now a rarity, or worse, face extinction. In my home county of Oxfordshire, sixty-three species of wildflower have vanished from our fields and woods in what seems like a blink of the eye.

But where there's life, there's always hope, and my wildlife garden is proof that nature has a remarkable capacity to regenerate itself extremely quickly. With twenty-four million gardens spread across our green and pleasant land – an area equal to a fifth of Wales – it's not hard to envisage what could be achieved, if we all become wildlife gardeners.

Together we could save the once-common turtle dove, the English bluebell and purple orchid from extinction, and see hares, hedgehogs, nightingales and barn owls return to the countryside. If we act now and act together, our summer meadows could murmur once again with soft, sibilant stridulations of crickets and grasshoppers and ring out to the melodious fluting of songbirds. Only then will our children, and grandchildren, wake to a world they deserve – a vibrant world awash with wonderful wildlife, just as I did all those many moons ago.

You may never know
what results come of
your actions, but if you
do nothing, there will
be no results.
Mahatma Gandhi

USEFUL BOOKS AND WEBSITES TO EXPLORE

Apart from my father's vertiginous pile of vintage nature and gardening books, I found the following websites and publications indispensable in the creation of my wildlife garden and writing *The Guilty Gardener*:

www.wildlifetrusts.org/wildlife gardening
www.rhs.org.uk
www.woodlandtrust.org.uk
www.habitataid.co.uk
www.meadowmania.co.uk
www.rspb.org.uk
www.plantlife.org.uk
www.davidaustinroses.co.uk

Frances Tophill: *Rewild your Garden* (Greenfinch, 2020)
The Butterfly Brothers: *Wild Your Garden* (Dorling Kindersley, 2020)
Kate Bradbury: *Wildlife Gardening for everyone and everything*
     (Bloomsbury, 2019)
Isabella Tree: *Wilding* (Picador, 2018)
John Lewis-Stempel: *Meadowland, The Wood and Still Water*
     (Transworld Publishers)

ACKNOWLEDGEMENTS

My thanks to everyone who has given me even the merest hint of encouragement along the way. I am profoundly grateful to my long-suffering husband, Ed, who weathered my dramatic highs and lows; my writing mentor, Janine Giovanni, whose guidance and unwavering support and enthusiasm gave me the confidence to write; the highly talented Iris Rushbrooke, whose exquisite illustrations brought tears to my eyes, and her equally talented sister Rose whose marketing ideas were invaluable; all my dear and loyal friends who volunteered to read and review my early drafts, mistakes and all: Phil Power, Sarah Rushbrooke, Seymour Banks, Claire Ellerton, Jeremy and Tessa Whitley and Sarah Prior. And thank you, Matthew Lagden, for stepping in and helping me with my limited IT skills.

My deepest gratitude to Miriam Murphy and all the wonderful staff and volunteers at the Berkshire, Buckinghamshire and Oxfordshire Wildlife Trust (BBOWT). You are an inspiration.

And thanks to everyone at Matador. It's been a pleasure working with you.

And, finally, but not least, Ron, and my amazing, naturalist father, who inspired my first love of nature. Also, my darling mother (who never doubted me – at least she never showed it!), Georgie, my devoted retriever and my greatest gifts – Olivia and Sam. Without you, *The Guilty Gardener* would still be a pipe dream.

Georgie